A Life of One's Own

A Life
of One's
Own

Individual Rights
and the Welfare State

David Kelley

CATO
INSTITUTE
Washington, D.C.

Library of Congress Cataloging-in-Publication Data

Kelley, David, 1949—
A life of one's own : individual rights and the welfare state /
  David Kelley.
    p.   cm.
  Includes bibliographical references (p. 153-167) and index.
  ISBN 1-882577-70-1 (cloth). — ISBN 1-882577-71-X (pbk.)
    1. Welfare state—Moral and ethical aspects   2. Public welfare—
Moral and ethical aspects.   3. United States—Social policy.
4. Objectivism (Philosophy)   I. Title.
JC479.K45   1998
361.6′1′0973—dc21   98-37024
                                                                    CIP

Printed in the United States of America.

CATO INSTITUTE
1000 Massachusetts Ave., N.W.
Washington, D.C. 20001

Contents

Acknowledgments

This book, like most, has been the labor of many hands. Merrill Matthews, R. Shep Melnick, José Piñera, and Michael Tanner were generous with their time in talking to me about their published works. David Schmidtz shared with me research for his own book on welfare and commented on early versions of the manuscript. For their inventiveness in finding the sources I needed, I am grateful to my research assistants, Joanne Phillips and Michael Young, and especially to Roger Donway, who also vastly improved the manuscript with his detailed comments. I'm indebted to Jamie Dorrian for the patient hours she spent preparing the manuscript for submission, and to Elizabeth Kaplan, my copyeditor at the Cato Institute, for her meticulous work in preparing it for publication.

Above all, I want to share whatever credit this work may deserve with Ed Crane, Cato's president, who had the vision to commission it; with my editor Tom Palmer, who saw the project through with unfailing wisdom, encouragement, and wit; and to all the members of the Institute for Objectivist Studies, who made this work possible with their generous support.

1. The End of Welfare As We Know It?

Personal and Public Standards

In our personal lives, most of us realize that the world doesn't owe us a living. Whatever our individual circumstances, we know that we are responsible for doing what it takes to get the things we want in life. We're responsible for earning a living that provides for both current and future needs. We're responsible, not just for doing our jobs day by day, but for finding a job in the first place and for acquiring the knowledge and skills it takes to find a job. We're responsible, not just for paying current expenses like rent and groceries, but for saving some portion of our income for long-term needs like retirement and for unexpected ones like an incapacitating illness. We're responsible, not just for getting the kids on the school bus in the morning, but for making sure they are learning what they will need to know in life. And we're responsible for choosing to bear children in the first place, knowing the long-term commitment it involves and the investment of time and money we might have devoted to other pursuits.

Yet in our public lives we have accepted an obligation to provide food, shelter, jobs, education, pensions, medical care, child support, and other goods to every member of society. The premise of the welfare state—the sprawling network of programs for transferring wealth from taxpayers to recipients—is that the world *does* owe us a living. If someone is unable or unwilling to support himself, the government will provide food stamps, housing subsidies, and possibly cash assistance as well. If someone is laid off, the government will provide unemployment compensation. If an unmarried teenager has a baby she can't support, she is eligible for cash benefits, Medicaid, and other poverty programs. If someone fails to save for retirement, the Social Security system provides a pension and Medicare covers the doctors' bills. In those and other ways, the welfare state confers entitlements to goods independent of the process of earning

1

them. It elevates needs and downplays responsibility. The result is a public morality at odds with our personal standards.

In our personal lives we know that people sometimes suffer through no fault of their own. We recognize a place in life for generosity and mutual aid. If a stranger is hurt in the street, we call the ambulance and see to his needs. If a neighbor's house burns down, we do what we can to help. But we choose to do so voluntarily, weighing such needs against the other demands on our resources, and we expect some measure of gratitude in recognition of our help. If a stranger appeared at our door demanding a place to live, or help with his medical bills, or a contribution to his retirement fund or to his kids' education—if he demanded it as a matter of right, regardless of whether we were willing and able to help, and without any obligation to thank us for helping—we would take offense. We would recognize it as a monumental act of presumption.

Yet in our public life we accept such demands as a matter of course. The beneficiaries of social welfare programs, and those who speak on their behalf, put forward their needs as claims on the public purse, and thus on the productive members of society who pay taxes. Those claims are not always successful. They may be opposed for economic reasons; they may fail to win political support. But they are rarely challenged as illegitimate. The operating assumption in debates about social welfare programs is that the needs of recipients take precedence over the rights of producers: those with the ability to produce are obliged to serve, while those with needs are entitled to make demands. The result, once again, is a public morality at odds with our private standards.

Federal budget deficits, and comparable fiscal problems at the state level, have come to seem intractable because food stamps, Social Security, Medicaid and Medicare, public housing, unemployment compensation, and other benefits have been provided as entitlements. Casting those benefits as rights has bred intransigence among recipients and thus made the prospect of benefit cuts all the more difficult for legislators to contemplate publicly. When the Massachusetts legislature voted in early 1995 to cut welfare benefits and require that recipients work, for example, welfare recipients marched through the statehouse protesting the new restrictions.

The spirit of entitlement is not peculiar to poverty programs. In New York City, students dressed in black held a mock funeral march from Battery Park to City Hall to protest cuts in federal spending on student loans and grants. Speaking of Social Security, Norman Ornstein, a political scientist at the American Enterprise Institute, observed,

> Talk to almost any audience of elderly people, and it becomes clear that the widespread public view is that recipients are "entitled" to these programs—and any cutbacks or changes are thus illegitimate. . . . A capped entitlement, of course, is like a partial pregnancy; the cap or limitation becomes increasingly difficult to maintain because one either has a right or one doesn't.[1]

The concept of a right to the goods and services provided by the welfare state is the chief source of disparity between our private and our public morality. A right is something an individual can demand as his due without apology for asking and without gratitude for receiving. When that concept is extended to the provision of social welfare, the necessary result is to empower those who make claims on public provision and silence those who do the providing. Since the New Deal, and especially during the three decades since the creation of the Great Society programs, the legal framework of entitlements has given rise to a public *spirit* of entitlement, a sense that the world does owe us a living.

Across its length and breadth, the welfare state is facing a crisis. In part, it is a social crisis, as the pathologies bred by dependence on welfare become more and more severe. In part, it is a financial crisis, as the costs of entitlements rise faster than the revenues available. At root, however, the crisis is moral—it is a crisis of legitimacy—and the fundamental issue in this crisis is whether people do indeed have a right to public support. Never before in the 60-year history of the welfare state have so many problems broken out across such a broad front. And none of the problems can be addressed coherently without tackling the fundamental issue: Do we have a right to be taken care of by others, or do we not? That question is the subject of this book.

What Is the Welfare State?

The welfare state does not consist solely of aid to the poor. It includes a vast array of programs through which the government transfers wealth among citizens. It includes Medicare, which pays

3

medical bills for virtually everyone over the age of 65. It includes workers' compensation and unemployment insurance, which cover most working people. It includes programs at all levels of government, from homeless shelters in the cities to the massive federal Social Security program. In one way or another, it touches the lives of virtually every member of society. Welfare spending accounts for about half of all government expenditures, far more than defense, the police and courts, or any other function.[2] All told, it involves the redistribution of about a sixth of the national economy.

The welfare state is a creature of the 20th century, at least in the United States. Cities and states had always had some sort of provision for the poor, including cash relief and the workhouse, but they didn't spend much money on those things, and the federal government was not involved at all. In 1930 governments at all levels spent $8 billion (measured in 1995 dollars), about 1 percent of the gross national product, on all welfare programs. By 1990 the sum had grown to nearly $900 billion, or 13.4 percent of GNP.

The first wave of expansion came in the 1930s with the New Deal measures instituted by President Franklin D. Roosevelt. Most of the money spent during that decade went for temporary public aid programs to address problems of poverty during the Great Depression. But the major welfare legislation of the decade, the Social Security Act of 1935, had a much longer term impact. It created Aid to Dependent Children, later renamed Aid to Families with Dependent Children, a national system of support for families in which the fathers were dead, disabled, or absent. The act also created a state-federal system of unemployment insurance. And of course it created the Social Security system for retired people. AFDC was a form of *public aid*, a term used to describe means-tested programs for which low income is a requirement for eligibility. Programs in this category provide aid for the poor; they represent a downward transfer of wealth from the middle and upper classes to the poor. Unemployment insurance and Social Security, on the other hand, are open to all classes. They are called *social insurance* programs because they are intended to protect working people, who can otherwise support themselves, against the risks of layoffs, injuries, and sickness and to provide retirement income. Social insurance programs transfer wealth in various directions: from the young to the elderly, from the well to the sick, and so forth.

The 1960s brought Medicaid and Medicare, which pay physicians' and hospital bills; Medicaid is a means-tested program for the poor, Medicare a social insurance program available to all retirees. These new forms of welfare were fiercely contested—especially Medicare, which covers many more people—because doctors feared that if government paid the bills it would soon begin exerting control over their profession. (As we will see in Chapter 4, that fear was amply warranted.) At the same time, the War on Poverty enlarged the welfare rolls by liberalizing eligibility for some programs and introducing new ones like food stamps. Spending on public aid tripled during the decade and has continued to increase rapidly.

Figure 1.1 shows the growth in total social welfare spending between 1930 and 1990. Figure 1.2 shows what the same numbers mean in per capita terms, taking account of the growth in population. Despite the enormous growth of the economy, which has made it possible for more and more people to earn a more and more comfortable living, government spending on individuals—and of course the taxes it takes *from* individuals—increased from $66 to more than $3,500 (in constant dollars) per person over the period. Despite that increase, the poverty rate—the proportion of the population with incomes below the official poverty level—has remained at 13–14 percent since the early 1970s. It had been dropping steadily before that, from about 30 percent after World War II, but leveled off just as the Great Society programs began to take effect. Although it has spent trillions of dollars, the War on Poverty has not lowered the actual poverty rate (Figure 1.3).

But it has succeeded in creating perverse incentives for its clientele, creating an "underclass" mired in dependence, drugs, and despair. AFDC in particular was widely blamed for encouraging young women to have children out of wedlock. In 1960, 5 percent of all babies were born to unmarried women. In 1990 the figure was 28 percent. The vast majority of those children are born to mothers with low incomes, and many of them end up on welfare. That is especially true of teen mothers. Over half of all expenditures for AFDC, Medicaid, and food stamps go to families begun with a birth to a teenager.[3] While there is much debate about the strength of the causal link between welfare payments and the decision of poor unmarried women to have children, there is no question that welfare protects them—as well as the vagrant fathers of their children— from the consequences of their actions.

Figure 1.1
SOCIAL WELFARE SPENDING, 1930–90

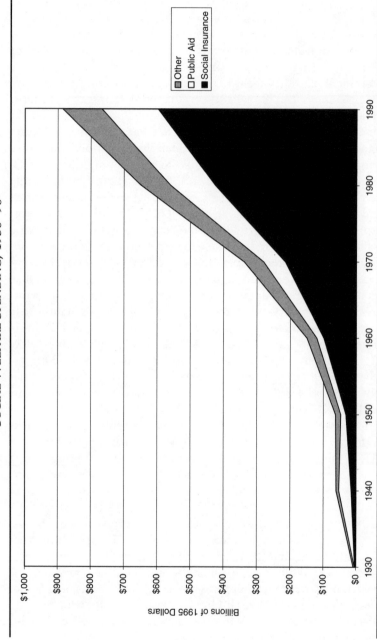

Billions of 1995 Dollars

■ Other
□ Public Aid
■ Social Insurance

SOURCES: U.S. Department of Commerce, *Statistical Abstract of the United States, 1997* (Washington: Government Printing Office, 1997), Tables 1, 576, 745; and U.S. Department of Commerce, *Historical Statistics of the United States: Colonial Times to 1970* (Washington: Government Printing Office, 1975), Series H 1–31.

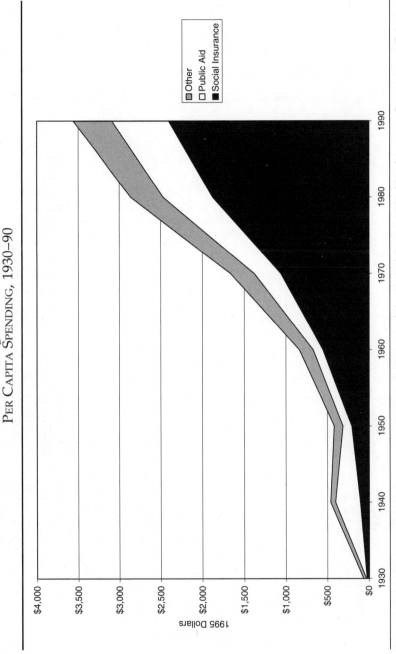

Figure 1.2
PER CAPITA SPENDING, 1930–90

- ■ Other
- □ Public Aid
- ■ Social Insurance

1995 Dollars

$4,000
$3,500
$3,000
$2,500
$2,000
$1,500
$1,000
$500
$0

1930   1940   1950   1960   1970   1980   1990

SOURCES: U.S. Department of Commerce, *Statistical Abstract of the United States, 1997* (Washington: Government Printing Office, 1997), Tables 1, 576, 745; and U.S. Department of Commerce, *Historical Statistics of the United States: Colonial Times to 1970* (Washington: Government Printing Office, 1975), Series H 1–31.

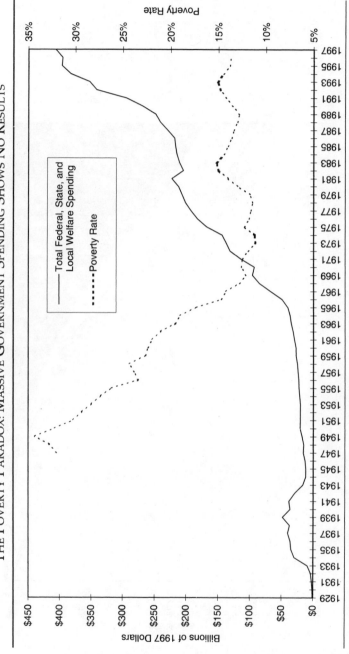

Figure 1.3
THE POVERTY PARADOX: MASSIVE GOVERNMENT SPENDING SHOWS NO RESULTS

SOURCES: Robert Rector and William Lauber, *America's Failed $5.4 Trillion War on Poverty* (Washington: Heritage Foundation, 1995), pp. 92–93, Table 1; Office of Management and Budget, *Budget of the United States Government, Appendix,* various years; and U.S. Department of Commerce, Bureau of the Census, *Current Population Reports,* Series P-60, various numbers.
NOTE: Accurate poverty data prior to 1947 are unavailable.

The larger problem, however, is that poverty programs as such dampen the incentive to become self-supporting through work. AFDC (now Temporary Assistance for Needy Families) was only one form of public aid, and not the largest. In 1994 AFDC spending ($26 billion) was matched by spending on food stamps ($27 billion) and Supplemental Security Income ($27 billion), a program for the disabled poor, and vastly exceeded by spending on Medicaid ($144 billion).[4] The package of benefits available through those and other programs, though not lavish, can easily add up to more than one could earn at a minimum wage job.[5] Over the long term, getting and keeping a job—any job, however ill paid—is an extremely reliable route out of poverty. In 1995 only 2.7 percent of people who worked full-time, year-round reported incomes below the poverty level.[6] The vast majority of people who start out in minimum wage jobs move up as they gain experience. But welfare discourages people from undertaking that arduous trek. The statistical consequence is that their incomes remain below the poverty line because they do not need income from work to provide for their immediate needs. The human consequence is that they become inured to a life of dependence.

The disability programs offer another example of perverse incentives. Until 1996 SSI was available to drug abusers and alcoholics, who were considered to have a disability. Though the recipients were supposed to be in treatment programs, that condition was virtually unenforceable; for many, the program was simply a way to have taxpayers support their habit. SSI benefits are also available to the parents of disabled children. A Supreme Court decision in 1990 required that "behavioral" disabilities, such as a tendency to be disruptive, be covered along with mental and physical problems.[7] The Court broadened the definition of mental disability to include mood and personality problems and to allow testimony from friends and relatives as well as medical evidence in establishing eligibility. As a result, there has been a gold rush among poor families to get their children classified as disabled; nearly a million children are on the rolls, up from 71,000 only 20 years ago.[8]

In the summer of 1996 Congress tried to deal with the social pathologies of welfare by enacting a major change in the system. In addition to trimming expected levels of spending for SSI and food stamps, the bill abolished AFDC. Previously, under AFDC, the federal government set rules on who was eligible for benefits and, in partnership with the states, guaranteed those benefits to anyone who qualified. Instead of those entitlements, the federal government will now send block grants to states to use for their own poverty programs, and the size of the grants is fixed. The law leaves states free to experiment with their own approaches to welfare problems but sets two important conditions: it requires adult recipients to find work within two years, and it sets a five-year lifetime limit on benefits to any individual. With all the loopholes, it's unlikely that the federal law will force anyone off the rolls, but many states are imposing more stringent rules, and news of the changes is deterring people from enrolling. The number of participants in AFDC, which peaked at over 14 million in 1994, fell to 12 million when the law took effect. When welfare officials in Creek County, Oklahoma, began publicizing forthcoming changes, and enforcing local rules on searching for work as a condition of benefits, the number of new applicants for welfare dropped by half.[9]

Poverty programs are the most graphic illustration of the incentives created by the welfare state. But those incentives are not confined to means-tested programs. Indeed, Medicare provides one of the clearest examples of what happens when government offers goods for free. James Weaver, a surgeon in North Carolina, tells of a 70-year-old patient who received $275,000 worth of hospital care, all paid for by Medicare, yet balked at having to pay $75 of his own money for a new set of dentures.[10] A primary reason for the rapid rise in Medicare costs is an increase in consumption of medical services by those who need not pay for them. When the program began in 1966, it cost $3 billion, and the House Ways and Means Committee estimated that the cost would rise to $12 billion by 1990, allowing for inflation.[11] The actual cost turned out to be $107 billion. The Medicaid program, even though it was intended for the indigent, is paying nursing home bills for many middle-class recipients: some 70 percent of the days spent in nursing homes are paid for by Medicaid,[12] despite the fact that only 13 percent of the elderly are poor.[13] There is now a flourishing Medicaid estate-planning industry to help elderly people divest themselves of assets and qualify as poor so that the federal government will pay the bills.

Although welfare is popularly associated with poverty, public aid programs directed at the poor represent only about 20 percent of total welfare spending, a ratio that has persisted since about 1950 (see Figure 1.1). By far the largest share of spending goes to the elderly, chiefly through Social Security ($340 billion in 1995) and Medicare ($180 billion). Both of those are social insurance programs, financed by payroll taxes and open to people who paid those taxes during their working lives. Having contributed to the system as taxpayers, retirees are partly justified in feeling entitled to their benefits. But the justification is only partial. Payroll taxes are often described as "contributions" paid into a "trust fund" and paid out later as "earned" benefits. In reality, payroll tax revenues from current workers are paid out to current retirees, and current workers will have to depend on the willingness of future workers to pay taxes for *their* benefit. As a result, there is only a tenuous relationship between what someone pays and what he gets. For example, someone who retired in 1980 got back in benefits all the taxes he paid, plus interest, in three years. Anything he received after that, or continues to receive, is a gift from the state. For those retiring in 1996, the payback period is 20 years; in 2025, when people now in their 30s retire, it will be 42 years.[14] Thus, the social insurance programs of the welfare state involve a mix of insurance and welfare.

As the nation ages, the cost of Medicare and Social Security will increase rapidly; the number of people receiving benefits will increase while the number paying into the system will decline. In 1960, for example, there were six people of working age (18–64) for every person over 65. By the mid-1990s there were only three workers for every retiree, and by 2020 there will be fewer than two. Medicare is already spending more than it takes in from the payroll taxes assigned to it, and the tide will turn for Social Security early in the next century. Younger workers are increasingly aware that they cannot expect all the benefits the system promises them—the money simply won't be there unless payroll taxes are raised to ruinous levels.[15]

The Crisis of Legitimacy

Many observers argue that the welfare state is here to stay as a permanent, ongoing feature of industrialized societies. "There is no escape in a modern developed nation," writes Harvard sociologist Nathan Glazer, "from the major social programs that were developed under Franklin D. Roosevelt and expanded in the years since."[16] Defending a conservative approach to welfare, Irving Kristol, editor

11

of *Public Interest,* asserts that "the welfare state is with us, for better or worse."[17] The answer to social and financial problems, according to this view, is piecemeal reform. Perhaps we can ameliorate the unexpected and untoward effects of welfare, but changing the system in more radical ways is impossible.

That attitude fails to recognize that the welfare state is a specific historical phenomenon. In its modern form it is just over 100 years old. During the 1880s, Germany under Otto von Bismarck created social insurance programs for old age, job-related accidents, and other medical costs. Great Britain began building its welfare state, partly on Bismarck's model, in the early years of this century. In the United States, as we've seen, the major welfare programs were created during the 1930s and the 1960s. Like communism, which once also seemed a permanent part of the political landscape but disappeared with astonishing speed when its historical moment passed, the welfare state may be nearing the end of its life cycle.

Communism collapsed when people stopped believing in the ideas on which it rested. The welfare state, too, rests on an idea. The thinkers and activists who built it insisted that the social provision of goods be treated as a right possessed by all people as citizens, rather than as an act of charity or noblesse oblige, a gift from some to others. A right is an entitlement, a possession of the individual. Providing medical subsidies, child support, Social Security checks, and the like as rights was supposed to provide recipients with dignity as well as security. But it didn't quite work out that way. Enacting entitlements to goods at taxpayer expense has produced exploding costs and a raft of perverse incentives. It is the concept of a *right* to such goods that gives rise to those and other ill effects. That concept has therefore been called into question by thinkers prepared to entertain more radical solutions to the problems of the welfare state.

The individualism inherent in the concept of a right breeds intransigence in those who claim rights to welfare benefits. In response to their claims, some commentators urge that we move away from the culture of individualism. "As various new rights are proclaimed or proposed," writes Mary Ann Glendon, "the catalog of individual liberties expands without much consideration of the ends to which they are oriented, their relationship to one another, to corresponding responsibilities, or to the general welfare." She goes on to note that a distinctive feature of "American rights dialect" is "its extraordinary homage to independence and self-sufficiency, based on an image of the rights-bearer as a self-determining, unencumbered individual, a being connected to others only by choice."[18] In a similar vein, Amitai Etzioni calls for a "moratorium" on the minting of new rights until some balance between rights and responsibilities has been established.[19] Thinkers of this persuasion normally argue, not that we should abolish welfare programs per se, but rather that we should make them more frankly paternalistic and communitarian.

Another school of thought, libertarianism, holds that welfare programs should be replaced altogether with private, voluntary efforts. Fifteen years ago, in a powerful critique of Great Society poverty programs, Charles Murray called for an end to such programs.[20] Since then the well-publicized financial problems of Social Security have led to a growing interest in privatizing the system, a proposal made prominent by the Cato Institute. Unlike communitarians, libertarian thinkers embrace the individualism inherent in the classical rights to life, liberty, and property enshrined in 18th-century proclamations on the rights of man.

Libertarians also distinguish sharply between political and civil society. Government is one social institution among many, an institution of a particular type. Its essential instrument is coercion: the power to raise money by taxes and regulate behavior by laws and regulations. Its use of that power is normally dictated by the political struggle among interest groups and causes. Its social welfare programs give money automatically to those meeting certain criteria. Civil society, by contrast, is the dense network of voluntary associations, and libertarians believe its instruments of mutual aid can be much more diverse and responsive to real needs.

The obvious social and financial problems of the welfare state are severe enough to call into question its very legitimacy, which rests on the concept of welfare rights. If entitlement spending is out of control, if the spirit of entitlement is poisoning our society, it behooves us to ask whether people really have the entitlements claimed on their behalf: What is the rationale for ascribing such rights to people? What assumptions do we have to make about human beings, as individuals and as members of society? What assumptions do we have to make about our moral obligations to each other? What implications does the concept of welfare rights have for the powers and responsibilities of government? How did the concept emerge historically? How do welfare rights relate to the traditional American rights of life, liberty, and the pursuit of happiness? Those are the issues I will examine in the following pages.

2. What Is a Welfare Right?

The Heritage of Rights

The United States was founded on the principle of individual rights. The idea of rights is more fundamental even than the idea of democracy, for the Constitution guarantees rights to individuals that the majority may not infringe, and the Founders adopted democratic procedures not as ends in themselves but as means for protecting the individual rights that were the real ends of government.[1]

In the 200 years of the American experiment, this country's commitment to individual rights as the foundation of government has been widely imitated. Particularly since World War II, the principle of rights has become an international standard for political legitimacy, embodied in the United Nations Declaration of Human Rights and other documents. Even governments that routinely violate the rights of their citizens find it necessary to cover up, make excuses, or claim that their actions reflect a "higher" concept of rights.

Even so, America remains unique in the role that rights play in its national culture. Unlike the countries of Europe, from which Americans inherited many of their ideas, and unlike emerging countries elsewhere that have tried to create a political order on the American model, the American nation is not rooted in ancient ties of custom, blood, and language. It was formed at a particular moment in time, by an agreement to live by the principles enunciated in the Declaration of Independence.

It is the very commitment to *principles* as the basis of political unity, rather than to the concrete emblems of ethnicity, that makes our political culture distinctive. It is this commitment that has allowed the United States to accept and assimilate wave upon wave of immigrants with diverse religions, languages, customs, and habits. As Allan Bloom noted in *The Closing of the American Mind,*

> by recognizing and accepting man's natural rights, men
> found a fundamental basis of unity and sameness. Class,
> race, religion, national origin or culture all disappear or

15

> become dim when bathed in the light of natural rights, which
> give men common interests and make them truly brothers.
> The immigrant had to put behind him the claims of the Old
> World in favor of a new and easily acquired education. This
> did not necessarily mean abandoning old daily habits or
> religions, but it did mean subordinating them to new
> principles.[2]

Those principles represented the flowering of Enlightenment
thought, specifically of Enlightenment individualism. The Declaration of Independence maintained that individuals possess certain
rights, that those rights are part of a higher law to which government
must submit, and that the purpose of government is to preserve
and protect those rights. Those tenets were rooted in an underlying
conception of the individual as the basic unit, the point of departure
for political analysis, and of social institutions as instruments for
serving individual needs. "Does man exist for the sake of government?" asked James Wilson, one of the authors of the Constitution
and a member of the original Supreme Court, "[o]r is government
instituted for the sake of man?"[3] He went on to express astonishment
that the former alternative had ever been seriously entertained.

But the individualism of the Enlightenment went deeper. It was
not merely the idea that government is the servant of the people,
an agent for meeting the needs of individuals. It was also the idea
that the individual's primary need is for liberty: the freedom to act
without interference, to be secure against assault on his person or
property, to think and speak his mind freely, to keep the fruits of
his labor. And while government is necessary to secure that freedom,
it is also the greatest danger to it. Thus, the concept of rights served
two functions in the political theory of the Enlightenment: to legitimate government and to control it. On the one hand, as John Locke
said, men consent to be governed in order to secure their rights;
that is the justification for the existence of government as an institution. On the other hand, the legal theorists of the 18th century insisted
on constitutions that limit the power of government and on bills of
rights to protect individuals against government encroachment on
their liberties.

It is against that background that we must understand the concept
of welfare rights, a concept that reflects a more expansive view of
the role of government than anything envisioned by the classical

liberals of the Enlightenment. "For Jefferson, . . . the poor had no right to be free from want," observes legal scholar Louis Henkin. "The framers saw the purposes of government as being to police and safeguard, not to feed and clothe and house."[4] Nevertheless, by asserting that people have a right to food, clothing, shelter, and other goods, the modern liberal architects of the welfare state were asserting a continuity with the classical liberal heritage. They were attempting to cast the new functions of government within established political and legal principles—in particular, the principle that the function of government is to protect individual rights. Our first task therefore is to sort out the new from the old and to define as precisely as possible what is meant by the assertion that the services of the welfare state constitute rights. In particular, we must distinguish the various levels at which welfare rights can be asserted and protected within the legal order, and we must understand the ways in which welfare rights to food, income maintenance, and other goods differ in content from the classical rights to liberty.

Statutory versus Constitutional Rights

The various programs that make up the welfare state give recipients *statutory* rights to certain benefits. Anyone who has paid Social Security taxes and applied for benefits upon retirement has a right to those benefits in accordance with the law. Families whose incomes fall below a certain level have a right to receive food stamps. On the other hand, adults who do not qualify for Medicaid or Medicare (or for any of the smaller government programs providing health care) do *not* have a statutory right to comprehensive health care, because Congress has not created a program to provide such care.

Statutory welfare rights come in various forms. Some are created by state laws, others by federal laws, others by programs administered jointly by the state and federal governments. At the federal level, the major division is between discretionary welfare spending and entitlements. Discretionary programs require annual appropriations by Congress, which decides how much money will be spent in a given year, and the amount that qualified recipients receive is determined by what's available. In the case of entitlements, the relevant statute defines a certain benefit for a certain category of persons, and Congress must appropriate enough money each year to provide that benefit for everyone who qualifies. Thus Aid to

17

Families with Dependent Children used to be an entitlement program: a cash grant per child was given to any unmarried woman with income below the poverty level. But the welfare reform of 1996 eliminated the entitlement, and cash grants became a matter of discretionary spending. The General Accounting Office notes that "authorizations for entitlements constitute a binding obligation on the part of the Federal Government, and eligible recipients have legal recourse if the obligation is not fulfilled."[5]

What Congress can give, however, it can take away. Even entitlements can be altered by a change in legislation. In 1970 the Senate Finance Committee asserted emphatically:

> Welfare is a statutory right, and like any other statutory right, is subject to the establishment by Congress of specific conditions and limitations which may be altered or repealed by subsequent congressional action. . . . The "right to welfare" implies no vested, inherent or inalienable right to benefits. It confers no constitutionally protected benefits on the recipient. To the contrary, the right to welfare is no more substantial and has no more legal effect, than any other benefit conferred by a generous legislature. . . . It is the ability to change the nature of a statutory right which distinguishes it from a property right or any other right considered inviolable under the Constitution.[6]

In rejecting the claim that welfare is a *constitutional* right, the Senate was opposing a widespread movement spawned by the War on Poverty of the 1960s. Social workers for the federal Office of Economic Opportunity were actively enrolling poor people in poverty programs. The National Welfare Rights Organization, with 20,000 members nationwide, was sponsoring marches, protests, and legal campaigns to expand welfare benefits. Free legal counsel was provided by the federal Legal Services Corporation. And the Center on Social Welfare Policy and Law, under the direction of Edward Sparer, was pursuing a systematic legal strategy to get welfare recognized as a constitutional right.[7]

The poverty lawyers won several important victories. In *Shapiro v. Thompson*, the Supreme Court struck down laws in Connecticut and elsewhere that denied AFDC benefits to poor families who had lived in the state less than a year; residency requirements, the Court held, unreasonably restrict the right to travel and thus deny to poor

18

families the equal protection of the laws.[8] In *Goldberg v. Kelly*, the Court ruled that welfare benefits cannot be terminated until after a hearing. Justice William J. Brennan's majority opinion cited the controversial theory of Charles Reich, a Yale law professor, that benefits from the government constitute a new kind of property and thus cannot be taken away without "due process of law."[9]

Edward Sparer hoped that the due process and equal protection clauses could be used to establish a constitutional "right to live"— a substantive right to receive welfare benefits—but the Court has refused to go that far. If Congress creates a welfare program, then the procedures by which benefits are determined and dispensed must satisfy constitutional requirements. For example, the welfare agencies cannot discriminate on the basis of race. But Congress is not required to create or maintain welfare programs in the first place. A 1976 Court opinion asserted, for example, that "welfare benefits are not a fundamental right, and neither the State nor Federal Government is under any sort of constitutional obligation to guarantee minimum levels of support."[10]

Even in regard to procedural issues concerning welfare, the Court has taken a narrow view of constitutional rights in the two and a half decades since the *Goldberg* decision. For example, AFDC benefits normally increased with the number of children in a family, but some states set an upper limit on benefits. And recent changes in federal law have allowed states to refuse additional benefits for children born while the mother is on welfare. The Court has consistently rejected the arguments of poverty lawyers that such restrictions violate the equal protection clause. Indeed, in the earliest of these cases, decided the same year as *Goldberg*, the Court said that "the intractable economic, social, and even philosophical problems presented by public welfare assistance programs are not the business of the Court."[11]

Although some legal theorists continue to believe that a constitutional case for welfare rights can be salvaged,[12] the judgment of Louis Henkin seems conclusive: "The United States is a welfare state by grace of Congress. . . . In constitutional principle Congress could, probably, abolish the welfare system at will, and the states could probably end public education."[13]

Welfare as a Human Right

Constitutional rights are the most fundamental level of our legal system, but they are not the deepest level at which we speak of

19

rights. For we also employ the concept of human or *moral* rights that we possess simply as human beings. A moral right is a principle stating what actions people *ought* to be free to take, or what goods they *should* be provided with—a principle, in other words, that sets a standard for government, whether or not a particular government meets that standard. The United Nations Universal Declaration of Human Rights, for example, lists a series of rights that it says the governments of the world ought to respect, whether or not they actually do so.

In this sense, it is legitimate to say that when a dictatorship imprisons a journalist for an article critical of the regime, it has violated the journalist's moral right to freedom of speech, even if that country's legal order provides no constitutional or statutory right to such freedom. In the same way, when advocates of universal health care speak of a right to health care, they are speaking at a level more fundamental than existing laws. They are saying that the government ought to create a legal entitlement to health care because there is an underlying moral right to that good.

At this fundamental level of basic human rights, the concept of welfare rights long predates the 1960s. In a book published in 1850, for example, Horace Greeley spoke of a right to a job with an adequate wage.[14] More to the point, the chief architect of the American welfare state, Franklin Delano Roosevelt, called repeatedly for recognition of rights to economic goods. "[T]he task of Government," he said in a 1932 campaign speech, "is to assist the development of an economic declaration of rights, an economic constitutional order."[15] At the end of his third term in office, he called on Congress to implement an "economic Bill of Rights," including rights "to a useful and remunerative job," "to earn enough to provide adequate food and clothing and recreation," "to a decent home," "to adequate medical care," and to "a good education," among others.[16]

The concept of rights to such goods was an essential element in the climate of opinion that made possible the creation of the welfare state during the 20th century. Such rights were constantly invoked by advocates of welfare programs as a rationale for government action. That was especially true in Britain and the United States, where the concept of individual rights was most deeply embedded in legal and political institutions, but the influence of the concept was much broader. Indeed, it is incorporated in the United Nations

Universal Declaration of Human Rights, which has been widely accepted as a standard for all nations. The first 21 articles of the declaration proclaim civil and political rights of the type our own Constitution protects: life, liberty, and property; due process and equal protection of laws; freedom of speech, press, and religion. But the remaining articles proclaim rights to food, shelter, education, and other such goods. As James Nickel observes, "These rights assert, in effect, that all people have rights to the services of a welfare state."[17]

Nevertheless, just as the idea of a constitutional right to welfare is at odds with the Founders' legal conception of the function of government, so the idea of a basic human right to welfare is at odds with the Founders' *philosophical* conception of the rights of the individual. Welfare rights are radically different from, and incompatible with, the classical rights to life, liberty, and property. Though the concept of welfare rights may be taken for granted by many people today, it reflects a profound philosophical change in social thought that has occurred over the course of the last 150 years. I will examine this change in the next chapter. To appreciate the magnitude of the change, however, it is necessary to understand the substantive differences between the two types of rights.

Welfare Rights versus Liberty Rights

Every right involves some claim that one person or group is entitled to make on others. It is this element—the moral claim at the heart of any right—that gives rights their special character. As philosopher Joel Feinberg puts it,

> Rights are not mere gifts or favors, motivated by love or piety, for which gratitude is the sole fitting response. A right is something a man can stand on, something that can be demanded or insisted upon without embarrassment or shame. When that to which one has a right is not forthcoming, the appropriate reaction is indignation; when it is duly given, there is no reason for gratitude, since it is simply one's own or one's due that one received.[18]

The dignity inherent in claiming one's rights is a primary reason welfare advocates have insisted on treating benefits as rights rather than as charity.

Welfare rights differ from the classical rights to life, liberty, and property in the nature of the claim that they embody. They differ in what is being claimed as a right, in the obligations that they impose, and in the way they are implemented. Those distinctions will help us define more clearly the principles that underlie the welfare state.

The primary difference is one of content, a difference in what it is that people are said to have a right *to*. The classical rights are rights to freedom of action, whereas welfare rights are rights to goods. That distinction has often been described as the difference between "freedom from" and "freedom to." The classical rights guarantee freedom from interference by others—and may thus be referred to as liberty rights—whereas welfare rights guarantee freedom to have various things that are regarded as necessities. What that means, in essence, is that the classical liberty rights are concerned with processes, whereas welfare rights are concerned with outcomes.

Liberty rights set conditions on the way in which individuals interact. Those rights say that we cannot harm, coerce, or steal from each other as we go about our business in life, but they do not guarantee that we will succeed in our business. Thus, the Declaration of Independence attributes to us the right to the *pursuit* of happiness, not to happiness per se. Society is responsible for ensuring the freedom to pursue happiness, but the responsibility for success or failure in that pursuit lies with the individual. Similarly, T. H. Marshall, a leading theorist of the British welfare state, noted that liberty rights "confer the legal capacity to strive for the things one would like to possess but do not guarantee the possession of any of them. A property right is not a right to possess property, but a right to acquire it, if you can."[19]

Welfare rights, by contrast, are intended to guarantee success, at least at a minimum level. They are conceived as entitlements to have certain goods, not merely to pursue them. They are rights to have the goods provided by others if one cannot (or will not) earn them oneself. Thus, they are quite different from the classical conception of rights as rules governing the *process* of producing the goods and services people want. Welfare rights require that the *outcome* of the efforts of productive members of society be distributed in such a way that everyone enjoys certain goods.

That distinction affects the meaning of specific rights such as freedom of speech. As a liberty right, freedom of speech protects a person from censorship and other forms of coercive interference with expression. It does not guarantee that he will have anything important to say, or that anyone will listen or agree, or that an editor will choose to publish his work, or that he will be able to afford a printing press or radio station; it merely guarantees that no one may forcibly prevent him from speaking. Many people, however, consider it a violation of their freedom of speech if they lack afford-able access to the media or if editors refuse to accept their work for publication.[20] That complaint treats freedom of speech as a kind of welfare right to certain goods.

The same ambiguity occurs even with the fundamental right to life. The classical right to life was conceived as a right to act with the aim of preserving oneself. It protects the individual from murder, assault, and other forms of aggression that threaten life. But it does not entitle the individual to the goods required to support his life, nor does it confer immunity from death by natural causes, even an untimely death. By contrast, Roosevelt held that the right to life included "a right to make a comfortable living."[21] In the 1960s, Edward Sparer's overriding goal was to create a constitutional "right to live," by which he meant a right to welfare benefits that are based solely on need and are large enough for a family to live on.[22] Roosevelt and Sparer were interpreting the right to life as a right to be provided with certain goods.

Negative versus Positive Obligations

One person's right always involves corresponding obligations on the part of others to respect that right. The moral claim inherent in a right would be meaningless if no one were obliged to respect it. Liberty rights impose on other people only the negative obligation not to interfere, not to restrain one forcibly from acting as he chooses. The negative character of that obligation was part of the classical conception of rights. "Mere justice," said Adam Smith, "is, upon most occasions, but a negative virtue, and only hinders us from hurting our neighbour. . . . We may often fulfil all the rules of justice by sitting still and doing nothing."[23] Writing about Thomas Jefferson's conception of rights, Daniel Boorstin noted,

> From his point of view the [Declaration] should have been
> considered a declaration of independence, not merely of the
> American colonies from Great Britain, but of each man from

23

all others. His "natural rights" theory of government left all
men naturally free from duties to their neighbors: no claims
could be validated except by the Creator's plan, and the
Creator seemed to have made no duties but only rights.[24]

In this framework, the positive obligation to provide another with
a good or service arises only from one's own consent or voluntary act.

But welfare rights impose on others positive obligations to which
they did not consent and which cannot be traced to any voluntary
act. If a person has a right to food, come what may, then someone
else has an obligation to grow it. If the first person cannot pay for
it, someone else has an obligation to buy it for him. A welfare right
is by nature a right to a guaranteed positive outcome that is not
contingent on the success of one's own efforts. It must therefore
impose on those who *can* produce the goods the obligation to
share them.

On whom does the obligation fall? Here is another point of difference between liberty and welfare rights. One person's liberty rights
impose on every other human being the obligation to respect them.
I am obliged not to murder or steal from other individuals, even those
I have never encountered and with whom I have no relationship. But
am I obliged to respect their welfare rights? No advocate of welfare
rights would say that a poor person has a right to appear at my
door and demand food, or a place to sleep, or any of the other goods
to which he is said to have a right. The obligation to supply those
goods does not fall upon me as a particular individual; it falls upon
all of us indifferently, as members of society. "[T]he moral obligation
to save any one person does not ordinarily attach to any other
particular person, it attaches to all members of the community collectively."[25] Insofar as welfare rights are implemented through government programs, for example, the obligation is distributed among
all taxpayers.

And that points to another aspect of the difference in obligations
imposed by the two categories of rights. The obligations imposed
by liberty rights are universal: one's right to life entails an obligation
on the part of every person, everywhere, not to murder, assault, or
otherwise harm him. But one's right to subsistence, education, or
any other welfare good creates an obligation only for members of
his own society. Some theorists, to be sure, have argued that these
obligations cross national borders, so that citizens of the United

States, for example, are obliged to support foreign aid for less developed countries.[26] But most theorists of welfare rights try to ground them in obligations associated with common membership in a community or nation.[27]

Some political theorists have challenged the distinction between negative and positive obligations on the grounds that even liberty rights require protection by the government in the form of police, courts, and other services. Liberty rights therefore impose on government—and thus, indirectly, on taxpayers—the positive obligation to supply those services.[28] But that argument fails to distinguish basic human rights from constitutional ones. At the fundamental level, rights are principles about the proper relationships among individuals—the claims they may legitimately make upon one another and the obligations they bear toward one another. At this level, rights exist regardless of whether they are implemented in the legal constitution of a given country. And it is at this level that the distinction between negative and positive obligations applies. Thus if the legal order does provide an affirmative right to protection of life, liberty, and property, the government's obligation is to enforce upon individuals their negative obligation not to interfere with one another. If there were a constitutional right to welfare, by contrast, the government's obligation would be to enforce upon individuals a positive obligation to support one another. The difference among rights, in short, would still exist.

As a point of fact, however, it should be noted that an affirmative constitutional right to government services does not always exist, even in the case of liberty rights. That affirmative right is recognized in the United Nations Covenant on Civil and Political Rights, which requires states "to respect and to ensure" the rights enumerated. The obligation to respect rights simply means that a government must not itself act in violation of the rights of its citizens, but the obligation to ensure their rights "implies an affirmative obligation by the state to take whatever measures are necessary to enable individuals to enjoy or exercise the rights guaranteed in the Covenant."[29] In the United States, however, the Supreme Court has consistently held that the Constitution does not impose any such obligation. The due process clauses, for example, "generally confer no affirmative right to governmental aid, even where such aid may be necessary to secure life, liberty, or property interests of which the government itself may not deprive the individual."[30]

Implementation

A right in the fundamental sense may exist whether or not it is recognized, protected, and enforced by government. But of course the whole point of rights is that they be implemented. To speak of a right is to speak of an entitlement (to an action or a good) that ought to be legally protected, and a corresponding obligation (negative or positive) that ought to be legally enforced. Liberty and welfare rights differ in the sorts of legal structures and government programs required for their implementation.

To implement the liberty rights of individuals, government must protect them against incursions by other individuals. That requires a criminal code with penalties for murder, assault, rape, theft, and the like; a civil code and courts for settling private disputes over property, contracts, and torts; and constitutional measures to keep the government itself from infringing on the rights of citizens. The laws involved are relatively simple; they essentially prohibit specific types of actions. The government apparatus required is relatively small, the "night-watchman state" of classical liberalism. The only significant expense involved is that of the military, to protect against foreign aggression.

The implementation of welfare rights requires a much more activist form of government. The welfare state typically involves large-scale transfer programs of three broad types, through which wealth is transferred from taxpayers to those on whom the state confers entitlements to various goods:

- Means-tested grants of cash or goods to those whose income falls below a specified level. Examples include Temporary Assistance to Needy Families (the basic welfare cash grant program, formerly AFDC), food stamps, public housing, and Medicaid.
- Socialized enterprises, in which the government has nationalized an industry (or at least is the dominant "firm") and made the product universally available. Public education is the chief example in the United States. In some countries, the health care system has also been nationalized.
- Social insurance, for which the government collects "premiums" as taxes and then pays out benefits. The chief examples in the United States are Old-Age and Survivors and Disability

Insurance (Social Security), Medicare, and unemployment compensation. Once again, many countries provide national health insurance to all citizens through government agencies.

The amount of wealth transferred in those ways is substantial. In 1992 total spending on social welfare, excluding education and veterans' benefits, by government at all levels in the United States was $936 billion, whereas the justice system (police, courts, and prisons) cost $94 billion and the military cost $298 billion.[31] In addition, the administration of the transfer programs is enormously complex by contrast with the relatively simple prohibitions involved in protecting the rights to life, liberty, and property. The welfare state involves government in running large-scale business enterprises: pension plans, health insurance, and so on. A complex set of regulations is required to define the entitlements of people, depending on the diverse circumstances of their lives, and a large bureaucracy is required to enforce those regulations.

Liberty and welfare rights differ, finally, in the level at which it is possible to implement them. The economic and technological development of a society affects the degree to which it can provide welfare rights to its members. A preindustrial society obviously cannot guarantee access to modern medical equipment and procedures. Even in a wealthy society, the potential demand for goods like health care or insurance against economic risks is open-ended. If individuals have rights to at least minimum levels of such goods, then the political process must decide what constitutes the minimum, the level that represents need rather than luxury. There is no universal and nonarbitrary standard for distinguishing need from luxury and thus for defining the content of welfare rights. It depends on the level of wealth in a given society.

The implementation of liberty rights, however, is not historically relative in the same way. The protection of an individual's liberty rights requires that other individuals, and the government itself, refrain from forcibly harming or constraining him or appropriating his property. The ability to forbear such actions is not a function of wealth. Of course, the protection of these rights in practice requires the existence of police, courts, prisons, and other elements of a functioning legal system. No society is willing to pay for enough policemen and prisons to wipe out crime entirely.[32] In that respect, liberty rights like welfare rights will not be implemented as fully as some people might like.

But the essential difference remains: the limits on implementing liberty rights are a function, not of a society's wealth in absolute terms, but of its willingness to devote some *portion* of its wealth to diminishing the risk of crime. Thus, the right to life may well have been as secure in colonial America as it is today, whereas it would have been economically impossible for colonial America to provide every youth with the right to 12 years of schooling at the taxpayers' expense, and technologically impossible to provide an entitlement to kidney dialysis or polio vaccination.

Conclusion

The differences between liberty and welfare rights in content, obligations, and manner of implementation make it clear that they reflect two radically different viewpoints about the moral relationships of individuals to one another and to society. The classical rights are an expression of Enlightenment individualism; their function is to protect the individual's freedom from interference by others, including the government. Welfare rights, by contrast, are based on a concept of positive freedom to live and flourish in society, and they imply a much more active role for government.

Liberty rights leave individuals responsible for living their own lives and meeting their own needs, and they provide the freedom to carry out those responsibilities. Individuals are free to act on the basis of their own judgment, to pursue their own ends, and to use and dispose of the material resources they have acquired by their efforts. Those rights reflect the assumption that individuals are ends in themselves, who may not be used against their will for social purposes. Welfare rights are based on a conception of individuals as inextricably rooted in their communities, with rights to the resources of those communities. Such rights do not leave individuals fully responsible for achieving the things they need or want. Nor do they permit the kind of autonomy implied by the idea of individuals as ends in themselves. The resources of the community include the productive abilities of its individual members, abilities on which other individuals have enforceable claims.

In short, liberty rights reflect an individualist political philosophy that prizes freedom, welfare rights a communitarian or collectivist one that is willing to sacrifice freedom. How did the latter philosophy arise historically? And why did its adherents make use of the concept of rights, which was rooted in the individualist tradition, to express the new outlook? I will examine those questions in the next chapter.

3. The Emergence of Welfare Rights

It is often said that the welfare state emerged as a response to the harsher aspects of industrial capitalism. That claim is premised on a view of the Industrial Revolution as a period of economic turmoil and misery for the working classes: long hours and low pay in the new factories, the constant threat of unemployment, and crowded and unsanitary living conditions in the cities. The various programs that make up the welfare state, according to this account, were responses to poverty, industrial accidents, unemployment, and other obvious and wrenching problems caused by industrialization.

That account is less than a half truth, and the purpose of this chapter is to distinguish the part that is true from the part that is not. The welfare state did emerge in response to real problems, of which the two most important were continuing poverty among those left behind by economic progress and the new forms of economic risk that arose as the economic fortunes of individuals became bound up with national and international markets. But those problems were neither obvious in nature nor wrenching in scope, coexisting as they did with the tremendous abundance and opportunity that industrial capitalism created on an unprecedented scale. And both problems were being addressed by private, voluntary organizations well before government programs were conceived and enacted.

As the 19th century progressed, however, the dominant intellectual and cultural trends were increasingly hostile to individualism and capitalism. The most influential social thinkers advocated an ethos of collective action. They were philosophically opposed to the values of Enlightenment individualism: the pursuit of happiness, individual rights, the spontaneous order of the market, strictly limited government. They argued that the individual is shaped by and is often a victim of his economic environment, that liberty in the negative sense—the mere absence of coercion—is not enough to ensure human flourishing, that individuals should be called to a higher moral duty than the pursuit of self-interest, and that the government should be given new responsibilities and new powers to solve social problems.

It was the intellectual changes, not the economic changes per se, that gave rise to the welfare state. It was the intellectual changes that made social reformers prefer government programs to private ones for addressing such problems as existed. The intellectual changes crystallized in the new concept of welfare rights, a concept that attempted to give new content to the political concepts of classical Enlightenment individualism.

The Economic Revolution

Poverty and Economic Risk

Material conditions that we would now describe as poor were the lot of virtually all human beings throughout most of our history; in fact, most people have lived in conditions much worse than do the poorest today. We still speak the political language of John Locke and Thomas Jefferson, the language of rights, democracy, and the rule of law. But we would be shocked to find anyone living today in the material circumstances that were common in Locke's day, or Jefferson's. Things that we take for granted and that are available to even the poorest people—from indoor plumbing to anesthesia to television—were unknown then.

The Industrial Revolution marked a turning point in human history. For many contemporary observers who were offended by the grime and clamor of production and viewed the agricultural past with nostalgia, it seemed a turn for the worse. Friedrich Engels claimed that English workers in the preindustrial era "enjoyed a comfortable and peaceful existence. . . . Their standard of living was much better than that of the factory worker today [1845]." They "vegetated happily, and but for the Industrial Revolution would never have left this way of life, which was indeed idyllic."[1] But that romantic picture simply does not square with the facts.

Prior to the advent of industrial production, the number of people who could survive was severely limited by the agricultural capacity of the land. Population studies of England show that, until the middle of the 18th century, there was a normal long-term rate of population increase of from 0.5 to 1 percent per year. But the normal rate was interrupted and wiped out by periodic famines and epidemics.[2] For the period before 1800, the thesis that Thomas Malthus advanced in his famous *Essay on Population* was roughly true: a growth in population was associated with a rise in food prices and a fall in real wages, because the preindustrial economy could not expand its production by more than about 0.5 percent per year.[3] Additional population meant there was less per person.

Ironically, however, Malthus's theory was being falsified at the very moment he put it forward. In England, after 1800, a rapid increase in population was accompanied by falling prices and rising wages. The population, which had increased slowly to about 6 million in 1750, exploded to 18 million by 1850. Many of those people made their living in the new factories. They worked soul-numbing hours and lived in squalid, crowded tenements. Their lot was hardly enviable, when judged by the standards of today. Yet the central and undeniable fact about population growth is that those people were able to survive: a land that previously could support only 6 million people could now support three times that number. As F. A. Hayek noted, "The proletariat which capitalism can be said to have 'created' was thus not a proportion of the population which would have existed without it and which it had degraded to a lower level; it was an additional population which was enabled to grow up by the new opportunities for employment which capitalism provided."[4]

During that period, moreover, standards of living did rise. Working people were able to enjoy cotton clothing, sugar, tea, and other amenities made possible by growing production and trade. Over the course of the century from 1750 to 1850, while the population tripled, the standard of living of that vastly greater population had at least doubled.[5] "Perhaps for the first time in the history of any country other than a land of recent settlement rapid population growth took place concurrently with rising living standards. A basic feature of the human condition had changed."[6]

Growth continued during the rest of the 19th century. In England, the real income of workers doubled again between 1850 and 1900.[7] In the United States, both population and per capita income tripled during the same period.[8] Of course, that progress did not occur in a straight upward line; it was interrupted by wars and recessions. Nor was it uniformly distributed; some regions and industries fared better than others. Even at the turn of this century, the living conditions available to working people were austere by present standards, and their opportunities were restricted. By comparison with earlier centuries, however, their material welfare had increased immeasurably.

It was against that background of increasing wealth for an increasing proportion of the population that poverty began to seem unnatural, a problem to be solved. Alexis de Tocqueville noticed that effect during his visit to England in 1833:

> The progress of civilization ... brings society to alleviate miseries which are not even thought about in less civilized societies. In a country where the majority is ill-clothed, ill-housed, ill-fed, who thinks of giving clean clothes, healthy food, comfortable quarters to the poor? The majority of the English, having all these things, regard their absence as a frightful misfortune; society believes itself bound to come to the aid of those who lack them, and cures evils which are not even recognized elsewhere.[9]

Even the welfare-state advocate J. A. Hobson, writing at the end of the century, admitted that poverty had become a social issue in part because expectations had risen faster than actual improvements.[10]

The issue of poverty pertained to those at the bottom of the economic ladder, but another issue affected all working classes: the problem of *economic risk*. Throughout the 19th century, as standards of living rose, and as agriculture became more efficient and required fewer workers, people moved steadily from farms into cities and manufacturing jobs. By 1900, for example, in the industrial Northeast of the United States, 66 percent of the population lived in urban areas, as against 9 percent in 1800. Throughout the industrializing world, the proportion of workers employed in agriculture fell dramatically.

That trend was part of an economic transformation that reduced the natural risks of famine and disease. Economic growth provided abundant food at lower prices. It improved shelter, sanitation, and medical care. But the reduction in natural risks was paid for, in part, by taking on new economic risks. People were no longer so dependent on the cycles of weather and pests, of good harvest years and lean ones. But the price was dependence on economic cycles. New competitors in other countries, changes in consumer demand for a product, bank failures, and other economic events outside the worker's control could affect his ability to support himself. On the whole, of course, the exchange of natural for economic risks was a net gain, and it was a huge one, as reflected in life expectancies that were rising as rapidly as standards of living. But insofar as the risks arose from society, not from nature, they were regarded as a social problem. By the end of the 19th century, there was widespread interest in finding ways to protect against the risks of unemployment, industrial accidents, and incapacity to work due to sickness or old age.

Philanthropy, Self-Help, and Public Aid

The industrializing countries responded to poverty and economic risk with a mixture of private and public efforts. In England the public effort derived from the Elizabethan Poor Law of 1601, which mandated a compulsory system of poor relief throughout the realm, administered by parishes and paid for by local taxes. At the end of the 18th century, food prices were rising, and the Napoleonic wars soon caused further hardship. Relief was made more generous in 1795, the relief rolls swelled, and England soon had a "welfare problem" that sounds very much like ours.

Spending on public relief increased dramatically: from 1.5 million pounds in 1775 to 4 million pounds in 1800 and then to 8 million pounds in 1817—a growth rate much faster than that of population.[11] As in our own era, however, the concern about relief for the poor had as much to do with morals as with money. There was widespread concern that the availability of relief encouraged vice and that it was a disincentive to work, turning able-bodied poor people into "paupers" (the term for those who could not, or would not, support themselves). Tocqueville voiced the common concern: "The number of illegitimate children and criminals grows rapidly and continuously, the indigent population is limitless, the spirit of foresight and of saving becomes more and more alien to the poor."[12]

Those concerns led to the Poor Law reforms of 1834, which were based on the principle of "less eligibility." As explained by the commission that recommended the reforms, "Every penny bestowed, that tends to render the condition of the pauper more eligible than that of the independent labouror, is a bounty on indolence and vice."[13] The reforms limited the amount of relief and, for those capable of working, restricted it to the workhouse, whose grim prisonlike character was considered sufficiently unpleasant to discourage anyone who was capable of working. In that way, it was hoped, relief would be sought only as a last resort, and only by those who truly needed it. As the commission argued, "If the claimant does not comply with the terms on which relief is given to the destitute, he gets nothing; and if he does comply, the compliance proves the truth of the claim—namely, his destitution."[14] The effect of the reforms was a drop in spending: in 1871 the poor rates were the same as in 1817 even though the population had doubled.[15]

Poor relief in America followed much the same pattern. The colonies provided local relief on the British model, and those provisions were continued by the states after independence. In the early 19th century, concern about the burden of taxation and the moral consequences of relief led to reforms similar to those in England, including the workhouse. By the end of the Civil War, for example, 80 percent of those receiving extended relief in Massachusetts were in institutions.[16] Unlike England, however, the United States did not have a national policy mandated by the federal government, nor were there any federal programs for the poor. Indeed, in 1854 President Franklin Pierce vetoed a bill to subsidize institutions for the insane. "If Congress has power to make provision for the indigent insane," he explained, "it has the same power to provide for the indigent who are not insane, and thus to transfer to the Federal Government the charge of all the poor in all the States. . . . I cannot find any authority in the Constitution for making the Federal Government the great almoner of public charity throughout the United States."[17]

During and after the Civil War, government relief programs expanded at the local level, especially "outdoor relief" (benefits offered outside the workhouse). By the early 1870s, according to Marvin Olasky, one-tenth of New York City's population was receiving food from public storehouses.[18] But that trend produced a reaction against government aid. Critics charged that relief was given indiscriminately, both to those who could not and those who *would* not help themselves; that it discouraged work, savings, and responsibility in general; and that it encouraged a spirit of entitlement.

At the same time, because poverty increasingly stood out against the rising standard of living for all classes, the Victorian era saw a vast outpouring of private philanthropic activity. Charitable organizations proliferated in major cities throughout England and America. In 1869 the Charity Organisation Society was founded in England to help organize what was already a sprawling network of philanthropic efforts, and an American version of the society was founded soon thereafter. In 1870 private charities in London donated between 5 million and 7 million pounds, as against 1.5 million pounds in government spending.[19] In the United States in 1890, some 112,000 people were housed in private charitable institutions, as against 73,000 in public almshouses.[20] In both countries there were religious charitable organizations of every type, including inner-city missions and shelters. There were organizations like the Children's Aid Society in New York, which found foster homes for orphans. There were new institutions for the deaf, dumb, blind, and insane. There were charity wards in hospitals and "dispensaries," free clinics dispensing medical attention and drugs.[21]

The defects of government programs made apparent the virtues of private ones. Private charities could give aid, not as a right, but as an investment in the recipient that carried with it the obligation on his part to develop the habits that would make him independent. Charles Loch Mowat, grandson of the founder of the Charity Organisation Society in England, noted that the society had "a sternly individualist philosophy, and paid the poor the compliment of assuming they shared it."[22] Private charities could discriminate, in a way that government could not, between worthy and unworthy applicants for aid, distinguishing the innocent victims of misfortune and the struggling poor from those who were indolent, or criminal, or abusing drugs and alcohol.

The Associated Charities of Boston said in one report that public relief "created a dependent feeling, a dry rot, which leads the recipient of city bounty to look upon it as something due as a reward for destitution."[23] Mary Richmond, who was general secretary of the Charity Organization Society of Baltimore, noted that such relief is the least desirable form of aid because it "comes from what is regarded as a practically inexhaustible source, and people who once receive it are likely to regard it as a right, as a permanent pension, implying no obligation on their part."[24] As a result of that sentiment, outdoor relief was abolished in New York in 1874, Brooklyn in 1878, Philadelphia in 1879, and numerous other cities by the turn of the century.[25]

During the same era, in response to the problem of economic risk, workers were forming mutual-aid or friendly societies with names like Manchester Unity, the Foresters, the Hearts of Oak Benefit Society, the Order of Eagles. In America, those were often ethnic organizations through which earlier generations of immigrants helped new arrivals: the Belgium Society of Benevolence, the Chinese Hospital Association, the Irish Immigration Society, and many others. They were insurance societies, not philanthropic ones; their goal was to shield their own members against economic risk, not to give charity to others. Typical benefits were old-age, illness, and accident benefits; a death grant for funerals; and support for widows and orphans. The organizations' chief function was to pool risk: for an annual membership fee, members were entitled to disability benefits if they became unable to work, and funeral costs and support for their families if they died.

It was a period of great experimentation. Different societies offered various arrays of benefits, subject to various conditions, among which workers were free to choose. By the 1890s virtually the entire British workforce, including poor workers, who were most vulnerable to economic risk, belonged to friendly societies. Membership dues that covered death and sick-pay benefits were typically about one week's pay per year.[26] In America at least one-quarter of adult males were members of friendly societies, and some estimates place the proportion higher.[27] The Italians in Chicago had some 110 mutual-aid societies; the average cost of membership in the most popular, the Unione Siciliana, was $12–$15 per year, which entitled one to sick pay while ill and a death benefit of $1,000 for one's family.[28] (Average earnings in 1900 were around $500 per year.)

The mutual-aid organizations were not without problems. They often lacked professional management, especially the smaller cooperatives formed and run by the workers themselves. Actuarial data on morbidity and life expectancy were not as well developed or widely available as they are today. With life spans increasing rapidly, the data collected on one generation had limited application to the next. And because the societies were often formed around characteristics their members shared—a common trade or workplace, region, or ethnicity—they could not enjoy the benefits of spreading risk over a diverse population.[29] Such problems could be and were addressed through the growth and professionalization of the mutual-aid societies.[30] In addition, insurance companies were beginning to offer accident and health insurance. Before the voluntary forms of protection against economic risk could develop very far, however, they were preempted by government-run "social insurance" programs—the beginnings of the modern welfare state.

Birth of the Welfare State

The welfare state as we know it was born in Germany in the 1880s, when Chancellor Otto von Bismarck first put the concept of "social insurance" into practice. Social insurance was not intended as welfare in the usual sense. Its benefits were restricted to workers who "paid" for them through payroll taxes. The public was told that such mandatory programs were protection against the economic risks of becoming unable to work because of illness or accident, layoffs, or old age. In 1883 the German *Reichstag* passed a bill mandating national health insurance; it required workers and employers to pay a portion of wages into "sickness funds" that had already been created as private voluntary associations. Mandatory insurance for industrial accidents was added the next year. Old-age and disability pensions—the equivalent of Social Security in the United States—were enacted in 1889.

The public rationale for those measures was to protect the workers. Germany was rapidly industrializing at the time, and the social insurance programs were billed as a way to spread the costs of industrialization over society as a whole.[31] But Bismarck's motive was primarily political. He wanted to curb the growing appeal of socialist parties to the workers by preempting the socialist promise of state-sponsored benefits. He also sought to limit the growing independence of the industrial workers, who were forming mutual assistance societies, including the sickness funds, and were losing the spirit of deference to paternalistic masters.

Bismarck's goal, first and last, was to strengthen the state by breeding dependence on it. "I will consider it a great advantage," he said in a speech to the *Reichstag*, "when we have 700,000 small pensioners drawing their annuities from the state, especially if they belong to those classes who otherwise do not have much to lose by an upheaval and erroneously believe they can actually gain much by it."[32]

The newly unified Germany did not have a deeply rooted liberal, individualist, laissez faire tradition. The dominant political culture, represented by Bismarck, was that of Prussian authoritarianism. As Gaston Rimlinger notes, "In a form appropriate to new circumstances, Bismarck's social insurance continued the patriarchal tradition of the absolutist state."[33] The neoliberal thinkers and activists in Britain and America did not share Bismarck's Prussian aristocratic conservatism, but they did adopt the social insurance programs he introduced. And in a broad sense they shared his belief in the propriety and efficacy of government action.

When the Liberal Party came to power in England in 1906, it moved to create a welfare system on the German model. Winston Churchill, after visiting Germany as head of the Board of Trade, proposed "to thrust a big slice of Bismarckianism over the whole underside of our industrial system."[34] In 1908 Parliament adopted the Old Age Pension Act, providing pensions for the elderly poor. That was a poverty program rather than social insurance; it required a means test and was funded through general tax revenues rather than payroll-tax "contributions." (Old-age pensions were put on a payroll basis in 1925.) The National Insurance Act of 1911 created a system of unemployment insurance, applied at first to a few industries and gradually expanded. The same measure instituted mandatory "contributions" for health insurance. The Great Depression led to a further extension of social insurance under the Beveridge Plan, which created Britain's current welfare state, including its system of socialized medicine.

With the Social Security Act of 1935, the United States adopted social insurance programs that created federal pensions for the elderly and disabled; the act also created a system of unemployment insurance, operated through the states. Both were funded by payroll taxes. In addition, the act created a program of public assistance for unmarried mothers, the forerunner of the Aid to Families with Dependent Children (now Temporary Assistance to Needy Families) program. Though those programs were created in response to the shock of the Great Depression, the way had been prepared by a generation of social activists. Henry R. Seager, a Columbia University professor, and Irving R. Rubinow, an insurance company statistician, were tireless advocates of social insurance on the German model.[35] In 1913 the American Association for Labor Legislation held the first conference on social insurance; three years later a government commission urged Congress to create a system of compulsory health insurance.

Reformers also hoped to create a system of old-age pensions, and they claimed a precedent in the pensions that the federal government was still paying to Civil War veterans and their survivors. Over the preceding 50 years, Congress had continually expanded benefits under that program; by 1910 about 28 percent of men and 8 percent of women over 65 were receiving benefits. Some advocates of social insurance wanted to broaden the program to all workers as soldiers in "the army of labor." But they could not overcome the public perception that the pension was an earned benefit of men who had risked their lives for the nation, rather than aid for the economically distressed.[36]

More generally, the German model of social insurance inspired opposition by advocates of American individualism. At the 1920 convention of the National Association of Manufacturers, compulsory old-age and health insurance was denounced as "one of the vicious German ideas yet existent in this country." M. W. Alexander of the General Electric Company argued that social insurance was out of place in a country "founded to secure individual liberty of thought and action with opportunities for working out one's own salvation."[37]

The only welfare programs that enjoyed political success in the early part of the century were state-level pensions to aid widowed or abandoned mothers. Their success flowed from the growing power of the suffragette movement as well as the cultural expectation that mothers should stay home with their children.[38] By the late 1920s virtually every state had such a program. But it was only in the Great Depression of the 1930s that the United States followed Germany, England, and other European countries in creating a national welfare state.

The various elements of the welfare state, as it evolved in Europe and America, were directed at what were seen as the primary risks of life in an industrial economy, where one's welfare depended on income from employment. Those were the risks of disabling accidents on the job, sickness, old age, and unemployment. Those risks were different in character, and the differences affected the corresponding programs; private, voluntary efforts to protect against risks were more advanced in some cases than in others. In addition, there remained the age-old problem of the chronically poor.

Industrial Accidents. Industrialization brought with it new risks of disabling accidents in the factories, in the mines, and on the railroads. In the late 19th and early 20th centuries, liability for industrial accidents was shifted from the worker to the employer, who was thus made responsible for paying benefits to workers disabled on the

41

job.[39] As a result, employers had an incentive to obtain insurance against such accidents, and many were receptive to government-run workers' compensation, which limited their liability. In the United States all but four states had workers' compensation laws by 1930.

Sickness. As wages rose through the 19th century, workers increasingly had both the means and the incentive to insure against the loss of income from sickness. Voluntary mutual-aid societies provided sick pay for days lost to illness. In many cases, they also had contracts with doctors to treat their members, an arrangement that was a forerunner of today's health maintenance organizations. In Germany by 1880, on the eve of Bismarck's social programs, some 45 percent of the population were insured for sickness through "an extended network of sick funds and union insurances."[40] Friendly societies in England performed the same function for at least 75 percent of workers.[41] Although the government provided small subsidies, its main function was to compel all workers to make the same provisions for illness that the more responsible ones were already making for themselves. Apart from that paternalism, health insurance was a straightforward economic good that could be—and was being—offered on the market.

Old Age. A recent compilation of social indices notes that the average length of retirement is now 11.4 years, up from 0 years in 1870.[42] That statistic reminds us that retirement is a recent concept. Well into the industrial age, the expectation was that one would work until one died. In the late 19th century, however, improvements in sanitation and medicine were wiping out the infectious diseases like typhoid that killed quickly; they were replaced by the chronic illnesses of old age. As a result, more and more people were living past the age at which they were capable of working, and many of the elderly suffered acute poverty.

In England the finances of the friendly societies deteriorated from 1890 onward as many of the elderly were collecting what were in effect old-age pensions in the form of sickness benefits. The annual membership premiums charged by the societies were typically based on actuarial data from the middle of the century, but as life expectancy increased, the premiums were inadequate to cover expenses.[43] In America as well as England genuine pensions—intended for retirement rather than sickness—were just coming into widespread use. Some corporations had begun to offer pensions as an employee benefit, or to subsidize worker enrollment in mutual-aid societies, but such plans were few in number. In 1930 in the United States, about 15 percent of the elderly population had pensions.[44] Like health insurance, savings for retirement—whether in personal savings accounts, life insurance policies, company pensions, or other instruments—could easily be offered commercially, and those instruments were being rapidly developed at the time.

Unemployment. In principle, individuals can self-insure against involuntary loss of work by accumulating savings. Commercial insurance poses some unique difficulties: unemployment tends to come in waves, like an epidemic, as a result of economic cycles; and it can be hard to determine whether an individual's lack of work is voluntary or involuntary. Nevertheless, unions and corporations began offering such insurance as an employee benefit. In England at the turn of the century, union policies covered some 750,000 workers.[45] By 1930 in America perhaps 150,000 workers were covered by union or company plans.[46] Commercial insurance companies also wanted to enter the field, but most states prohibited them from doing so. Beginning in 1926, Haley Fiske, president of the Metropolitan Life Insurance Company, sought permission from New York State insurance regulators to offer unemployment policies. An authorization bill finally passed the state legislature in 1931 but was vetoed by Gov. Franklin D. Roosevelt, who "feared that the bill would preempt a regional conference of governors he was convening for the study of government UI."[47]

Poor Relief. As we have seen, governments had been involved in aid to the poor long before the industrial period. During the late 19th century, government relief was overshadowed by private efforts, but the tide soon turned the other way. Richard Ely, an economics professor (and one of Woodrow Wilson's teachers), who founded the American Economic Association, argued in a number of books that the exercise of philanthropy was the function of government.[48] The volunteer charity workers who operated under the aegis of the Charity Organizations Society and other groups were gradually replaced by professional social workers who lobbied for government support. Government relief increased gradually during the early part of the century,[49] especially, as noted above, in the form of state programs to support mothers, and was added to the federal government's functions in the Social Security Act.

The Intellectual Revolution

Anti-Individualism

The replacement of private efforts by government programs involved a sea change in thinking about the problems of poverty and economic risk. That change was not driven solely by events. It was the expression of a change in basic principles and values—an *ideological* change—on the part of social reformers.

Advocates of government measures often argued that private efforts had failed: they were not providing enough aid. But that claim is disingenuous. "Enough" is a normative term; it implies a standard. By historical standards, private philanthropy was at unprecedented levels. It cannot be emphasized too often that welfare is an issue of distribution, not production. A society cannot provide more aid than it can produce; government does not create wealth, it only transfers it. Workers at the beginning of the 19th century could not possibly have been given insurance benefits on the scale conceived at the end of the century. In most cases, moreover, social insurance was supported by payroll taxes, as a percentage of the workers' income—a percentage they themselves could have invested in voluntary systems.[50] The real meaning of claims that private efforts were not doing "enough," therefore, is that such efforts did not distribute benefits in the manner that reformers wanted.

It has also been claimed that the welfare state was the inevitable result of industrialization. That, too, is disingenuous. We have discussed the real problems that did arise as byproducts of industrialization. If industrialization had been a primary cause of the welfare state, however, one would expect England and America to have led the way in adopting welfare programs, since they were the leaders in industrialization. But England and America adopted welfare state measures *after* many less developed countries, such as Germany, Austria, Finland, and Italy, did so.[51] The culture of those countries was obviously more amenable to government welfare than was the culture of England and America. In the latter countries, the reformers themselves were conscious of fighting against an individualistic culture that believed in self-reliance and self-improvement, regarded the dole with disdain, and had created a network of voluntary institutions that were already doing much of the work the reformers sought for the state.[52] In England, as Bentley Gilbert observes, social legislation was a new issue in politics, outside the normal government functions of maintaining domestic order and conducting foreign relations. The impetus for change came from a cadre of ideologues, not from popular demand. "Welfare legislation never figured as an electoral issue in the years before World War II."[53]

No change in the conception of government's role as massive as the welfare state could be driven simply by economic facts. Any such change is a response to facts as interpreted in the light of prevailing assumptions. As the prominent egalitarian R. H. Tawney observed, "Social institutions are the visible expression of the scale of moral values which rules the minds of individuals, and it is impossible to alter institutions without altering that moral valuation."[54] The change in moral valuation—the change in ideas, values, and philosophical outlook—came about through the work of intellectuals and political activists who were vehement critics of individualism and capitalism. To understand the magnitude of that change, it is important to understand the outlook they were rejecting.

Although markets of some sort have always existed, the capitalist system of free markets was something new in human history. As a replacement for feudalism, mercantilism, and other systems that involved large-scale government control of economic affairs, capitalism was a product of the same Enlightenment philosophy of individualism that, as we saw in the last chapter, was the source of the classic conception of individual rights. At the foundation of that philosophy was the acceptance of self-interest—the pursuit of one's happiness, including material wealth and comfort—as a morally legitimate end of human action. The Enlightenment individualists also relied on reason, as opposed to faith or authority, to define self-interest and guide its pursuit. James Wilson, one of the Founding Fathers, explained the role of reason and self-interest in the classical understanding of natural rights:

> Nature has implanted in man the desire of his own happiness;
> she has inspired him with many tender affections towards
> others, especially in the near relations of life; she has
> endowed him with intellectual and with active powers; she
> has furnished him with a natural impulse to exercise his

powers for his own happiness, and the happiness of those
for whom he entertains such tender affections. If all this be
true, the undeniable consequence is, that he has a right to
exert those powers for the accomplishment of those purposes,
in such a manner, and upon such objects, as his inclination
and his judgment shall direct.[55]

In social theory, that philosophy implied a confidence in the spontaneous order of the marketplace. As Adam Smith had shown, there
is a natural harmony of interests among individuals freely pursuing
their own ends and interacting with each other by trade to mutual
advantage. The role of government in such a system was conceived
as limited, with few exceptions, to the protection of the individual's
right to pursue his ends, including the use of his property, according
to his own judgment.[56] The concept of rights, as we saw, was a
negative one: the right to be free from coercive interference with
one's freedom of action. That concept did not include any welfare
right, any entitlement to goods provided by others outside the nexus
of voluntary mutual exchange. Economist Nassau Senior, who
served on the Poor Law Reform Commission, was explicitly opposed
to any right to relief. The Poor Law, he argued, perpetuated medieval
serfdom: the price of guaranteed subsistence was the loss of liberty.[57]
The American sociologist William Graham Sumner opposed government relief as incompatible with a society of contract.[58]

Though the concepts of that classical liberal philosophy have
become part of our public tradition, the philosophy represented a
revolution in thought as profound as the political revolutions it
inspired. As a form of radical individualism, it opposed the status
orientation of the feudal and mercantile systems. The belief in the
individual's right to pursue his own self-interest was a rejection of
earlier views that morality revolved around the obligation to serve
tribe, city, country, or king. The belief in reason as a universal human
faculty, which gives everyone the capacity to govern his own life,
undermined the rationale for paternalism and authoritarianism,
which had vested wisdom in an elite.[59] Like the Industrial Revolution
in the economic sphere, this philosophical outlook represented something new in human history.[60]

The thinkers who came to oppose the Enlightenment outlook
during the 19th and 20th centuries presented themselves as innova-
tors, and in some respects they were. In fundamental terms, however,

they sought a return to older principles. The first and most extreme opponents of individualism and capitalism were the socialists, who sought to restore a communal ethic. Karl Marx wrote a vehement attack on the entire concept of individual rights and its individualist presuppositions, proposing to replace capitalism altogether with a collectivist system of production and distribution.[61] The full-blown collectivism of the socialists never took hold in Britain or America, countries with a strong individualist tradition. But thinkers like Thomas Hill Green and L. T. Hobhouse in England and John Dewey in America explicitly rejected elements of the individualist tradition, including the legitimacy of self-interest and reliance on the individual use of reason, and embraced some elements of collectivism. The result was a new outlook, called "the new liberalism" at the time but known today simply as liberalism. The anti-individualism of the new liberals involved five elements that together produced the new concept of welfare rights.

Positive Freedom

In the classical conception, freedom means the absence of coercive interference with one's actions. A free person is able to choose among the various opportunities for action that are open to him. The nature of those opportunities, however, is determined by his ability and circumstances and is not an issue of freedom. A person with greater intelligence, knowledge, wealth, or reputation has more opportunities—and more attractive ones—than does someone with a lesser degree of those assets. But in the absence of interference, both are equally free to choose among their options.

That classical conception was rejected, often with scorn, by the new liberals. What is needed, they said, is a positive conception of freedom that takes account of the opportunities a person has or lacks. That conception of freedom was earlier developed by philosophers such as Jean-Jacques Rousseau and Georg Hegel, but it was put to political use by the new liberals as a rationale for the welfare state. They were especially scornful when their opponents objected to the sacrifice of "negative" liberty through compulsory insurance, increased taxes, and other exercises of coercion by the state. To oppose welfare programs because they infringe upon the old-fashioned negative freedom of citizens, argued J. A. Hobson, "is to furnish the mere forms of liberty and to deny the substance.... Free land, free travel, free power, free credit, security, justice and education, no man is 'free' for the full purposes of civilised life today unless he has all those liberties."[62]

In the United States, the new liberalism in general and the concept of positive liberty in particular were advocated by John Dewey, Louis D. Brandeis, and other exponents of philosophical pragmatism. In an article on social insurance, for example, Brandeis argued:

> Politically the American workingman is free, so far as the law can make him so. But is he really free? Can any man be really free who is constantly in danger of becoming dependent for mere subsistence upon somebody and something else than his own exertion and conduct? Men are not free while financially dependent upon the will of other individuals. Financial dependence is consistent with freedom only where claim to support rests upon right and not upon favor.[63]

The most famous expression of the concept of positive freedom was Franklin Delano Roosevelt's "Four Freedoms" speech. The first two freedoms, of speech and of religion, are instances of the classical negative liberties, as is the fourth item on Roosevelt's list, freedom from fear of violence and aggression. But the third freedom, "freedom from want," means the enjoyment of various goods and services provided by society to individuals who cannot provide for themselves. In effect, Roosevelt was attempting to graft the services of the welfare state onto the traditional conception of American liberties.[64]

Economic Coercion

Accompanying the new concept of freedom was a new concept of coercion. "Freedom" and "coercion" are correlative terms. The first refers to a condition in which an individual has the capacity to act independently, the second to a condition in which independent action is impossible, in which the individual has been made involuntarily dependent on the will of another. Just as the new liberals expanded the concept of freedom to include the enjoyment of various economic goods, they employed an expanded concept of "economic coercion" to include deprivation of those goods. Coercion was no longer limited to the use of force by one individual against another or by government against citizens. It now included any action—by an employer toward his workers, by a business toward its customers, and even by the capitalist system as a whole toward everyone—

that the new liberals felt unduly restricted the weaker party's opportunities.

The English writer Herbert Samuels gave particularly clear voice to that conception:

> Because the law does not interfere with his actions a man is not necessarily free. There is economic restriction as well as legal restriction. If the tramway conductor agrees to serve twelve hours a day for thirteen days out of fourteen, we cannot say that, because no law compels him, he does this of his own choice. The industrial system irresistibly bends to its will all who form part of it; the workman must submit to the customs of his trade and workshop under penalty of dismissal; liberty to "go elsewhere" is an empty privilege when the conditions are everywhere the same; and the individual finds that he is hardly more free to decide, as an individual, the conditions of his own employment than a passenger is able to leave a train running at full speed or to alter its pace.[65]

In America the most common use of the new concept of coercion was to advance the claim that the major industrialists and financiers possessed economic power that was indistinguishable from political power backed by force. Dewey took it as a truth beyond argument that "the control of the means of production by the few in legal possession operates as a standing agency of coercion of the many."[66] Progressive politicians from Woodrow Wilson to FDR played on the same assumption. During his first campaign for the presidency, for example, Roosevelt drew an analogy between the ruthless political despots whom the classical liberals sought to curb by limiting their power and the equally ruthless industrialists. "Where Jefferson had feared the encroachment of political power on the lives of individuals, Wilson knew that the new power was financial."[67]

That expansion of the concept of coercion led by an ineluctable logic to the expansion of government power over the economy. The classical liberals of the Enlightenment era had established the principle that government must ensure individual freedom by prohibiting murder, assault, theft, and other criminal acts of force. The government must use retaliatory force to counter the use of coercion by one individual against another. The new liberals retained that principle but redefined its terms. The state, in their eyes, was justified

49

in using its coercive powers to combat the "coercion" exercised by banks, corporations, and others. "The function of State coercion," said Hobhouse, "is to override individual coercion."[68] That principle was used to justify a wide range of Progressive Era measures, from antitrust laws to legislation limiting hours of labor. But it also played a role in the growth of the welfare state, insofar as poverty and economic risk came to be seen as conditions that people were "forced" to endure by an uncaring system.

Environmental Determinism

Despite the claims of the new liberals, there is an evident difference between the power of a government to throw one in jail and the power of an employer in a free and competitive market to refuse one a job. The new liberals' refusal to accept that distinction may be traced to a third assumption. The doctrine of environmental determinism held that human beings are so shaped by their circumstances that they have no more genuine choice in the face of economic restraints and inducements than they have in the face of literal physical force. "The advocates of the welfare state," observes Norman Barry, "were able to argue that the individual had little or no control over his destiny in the context of impersonal market forces."[69]

The role that this assumption played in the growth of social insurance programs can be seen in a speech FDR made on the third anniversary of the Social Security Act:

> But as the Nation has developed, as invention, industry, and commerce have grown more complex, the hazards of life have become more complex. Among . . . the often intangible forces of giant industry, man discovered that his individual strength and wits were no longer enough. . . . The millions of today want, and have a right to, the same security their forefathers sought—the assurance that with health and the willingness to work they will find a place for themselves in the social and economic system of the time.[70]

In part, Roosevelt's argument is simply a recognition of a fact we have already discussed—that industrialization brought about the replacement of natural risks by economic ones. It is obviously reasonable for people to seek protection against such risks. But the insistence that protection be provided by the state, rather than by friendly societies, commercial insurance, or other voluntary agencies, reflected the assumption that individuals were not only confronted with new risks but were powerless in their face. Gertrude Himmelfarb notes that in late 19th-century discussions of social problems, terms that refer to people ("the poor," "the unemployed") were gradually replaced by terms referring to social conditions ("poverty," "unemployment"). "The emphasis thus shifted from the personal characteristics of the poor—their particular circumstances, characters, habits—to the impersonal causes of poverty—the state of the economy, the structure of society, the action (or inaction) of government, the institutions and forces affecting social conditions and relations."[71]

The explanation for that shift in perspective was a growing conviction by philosophers and social scientists that free will and individual autonomy are myths, that social forces govern not only the individual's external circumstances but his inner motivation and beliefs. Once again, the socialists took the extreme position. Marx held that the thoughts, convictions, and values of the individual are byproducts of the forces of production. But the new liberals sipped from the same stream of thought. "Coming to look at the attributes and actions of an individual," wrote English philosopher Francis C. Montague, "I find that these attributes are nothing more or less than the relations of the individual to other things. . . . [T]he individual, out of relation to other things, is literally nothing. . . . [E]very civilized man owes his character to his society."[72] John Dewey insisted that the conception of the individual as the captain of his soul was a delusion.[73]

The practical import of this doctrine was the view that people are essentially victims, without the inner resources to help themselves. The distinction between the deserving and the undeserving poor, which had been so important to earlier generations of philanthropists, was gradually abandoned. J. A. Hobson heaped scorn on the Charity Organization Society, which emphasized the inculcation of character as the fundamental method of helping the poor improve their lot. Character, he insisted, was itself the product of environmental factors; the poor could not be expected to acquire regular habits of work and thrift unless society guaranteed their economic security.[74] By the 1960s some activists were arguing that there should be no "penalty" for those unable to hold a job, since personality flaws are socially determined.[75]

The link between determinism and the expanded concept of coercion is thus clear. If human beings lack the inner resources to form their own values and convictions, if they are vulnerable to all the social influences acting upon them, then every such influence is in effect a compulsion, and there is no difference in kind between the literal use of force and the "forces" that were said to keep people from acting responsibly. That outlook was of course reinforced by psychologists such as Sigmund Freud and B. F. Skinner. Despite the differences in their views, Freud's psychoanalytic theory and Skinner's behaviorism agree in holding that our behavior is governed by forces outside our knowledge and control.

The ideas of positive freedom, economic coercion, and environmental determinism combined to form a picture of the individual as dependent, constrained, often victimized by social forces, and unable to pursue his own well-being without extensive help from the state. This change in intellectual outlook took place in defiance of the facts. It occurred at a time when the spirit of liberty had freed individuals to fashion their own lives and economic growth had created new opportunities on a vast scale. Industrial capitalism was providing ordinary people with more effective independence than they had ever known. Unlike his counterpart 200 years earlier, the average person at the turn of this century could choose among an array of trades and professions to support himself. He could travel beyond the immediate neighborhood of the town where he was born. And he was literate: a basic education, along with cheap newspapers and books, gave him access to a level of knowledge that only a few could attain in earlier ages. In short, the growing complexity of social life was a liberating force, not a constraining one. But the intellectuals of the time saw only constraints.

Altruism

The thesis of environmental determinism was a factual claim about human nature, put forward as the product of allegedly hard-headed scientific thinking about the causes of human behavior and character. But the new liberals also relied on a normative claim, a value judgment about the way people ought to behave. The normative basis for their belief in state-run poverty and social insurance programs was *altruism*, the view that self-sacrifice is noble, that individuals ought to live for the good of others. Owen Lovejoy, president of the National Conference of Social Work, asserted that "but one kind of sacrifice is justified in any scheme of divine government worthy to organize and rule this universe—namely: self-sacrifice."[76]

The earlier generation of philanthropists was inspired largely by religious motives. They too sought to practice the tenets of Christian charity. But they regarded that as a matter of personal virtue, requiring the individual's choice to help others and his personal involvement in charity work. The Victorian philanthropists retained the individualist idea that aid to others should be voluntary.[77] The new liberals, however, advocated a secularized version of altruism in which service to the state replaced service to God. Government welfare programs came to be seen as "the outer form of the altruistic spirit—the unselfish, loving, just nature of the new man."[78]

In an age when science and Biblical scholarship were breeding skepticism about the truth of religion, thinkers like Thomas Hill Green yearned for a way to preserve the ethical doctrines that religion taught. An Oxford philosopher whose students included Herbert Asquith, William Beveridge, and other architects of the British welfare state, Green asserted that "God has died and been buried, and risen again, and realised himself in all the particularities of a moral life."[79] The moral life, he insisted, required a willingness to submerge one's personal interests in the greater good of society. The positivist philosophy of the French thinker Auguste Comte, who coined the term "altruism," taught the same doctrine. Charles Booth, whose study of the poor in London was the most complete statistical body of information available in the late 1800s, declared himself a positivist, as did many of his peers. He defined the creed as meaning "that I worship Humanity. By humanity I mean the human race conceived as a great Being."[80] Beatrice Webb, the Fabian socialist, traced that brand of socialism to an intellectual milieu in which "the impulse of self-subordinating service was transferred, consciously and overtly, from God to man."[81]

This secular version of altruism, together with the view that the individual was socially determined, gave rise to the collectivist idea of the common good as something superior to the individual's good, and even to the sum of individual goods. The liberals of the Enlightenment had argued that social institutions, including the government, were instruments to help individuals in their pursuit of their personal ends. That individualist view was widely rejected by the new liberals as well as the socialists. Sidney Webb maintained that "social health . . . is something apart from and above the separate interests of individuals, requiring to be consciously pursued as an end in itself."[82] Psychologists and educators increasingly defined normality in terms of adjustment to the group. "At a certain level of intelligence a man must be social," wrote one psychologist, "because he perceives instinctively that he can only reach self-fulfilment through his relationship with the 'herd.' "[83]

The practical import of these strands of thought was that proposals for government action no longer had to be justified by appeal to the welfare of individuals. The welfare state is a mechanism for transferring money from person A to person B. In terms of individual welfare, B's gain is A's loss. But for the new collectivist outlook, there was also the higher good of society to consider. Rimlinger notes that the early advocates of social insurance in America

> discarded voluntary efforts and commercial insurance as being inadequate for the task and unsuitable for an object of overriding national significance. For it was not merely the interest and welfare of the individual that was at stake but the collective interest and public welfare of the entire nation.[84]

In the case of health insurance in particular, advocates of government programs argued that a healthy workforce was a national resource, important not only for domestic production but to supply troops for the military.[85]

Apotheosis of the State

The classical liberals were suspicious of government and dubious about its power to achieve benevolent effects. In their view, the function of government was to keep the peace and to provide "public goods," such as roads and a postal system, that were regarded as beyond the capacity of private enterprise. Government's function, in other words, was to create a framework within which individuals had the freedom, and the responsibility, to pursue their own welfare. The classical liberals supported a number of political devices—written constitutions, tripartite government, the federal system—to keep the state within its bounds. The new liberals completely abandoned that attitude, adopting a more sanguine and expansive view of government. "[T]he State has evolved from being the embodiment of force," wrote a British local official in a typical expression of the new attitude, "and developed gradually until in modern days it emerges as guide, philosopher and friend."[86]

The classical liberals had drawn a sharp distinction between society and state. "Society is produced by our wants and government by our wickedness," wrote Thomas Paine in *Common Sense*; "the former promotes our happiness positively by uniting our affections, the latter negatively by restraining our vices."[87] Society meant civil society, the network of voluntary associations that radiated outward from every individual: to his family, to his neighbors, to his employer and the people he worked with, to those who shared his religion or his interests in ideas, sports, charitable causes, and so on. Such common purposes formed the basis for a dense array of social organizations in which people came together voluntarily to mutual advantage, including the friendly societies, lodges, unions, and fraternal orders through which they sought protection from economic risk. These myriad relationships, in the classical liberal view, reflected man's nature as a social animal. As individualists, however, liberals regarded associations with others as instruments in the pursuit of individual happiness, sustained by individual initiative and entered into by individual choice, so that no two individuals exhibited the same pattern of associations. The political realm, by contrast, united everyone under the same government—and did so as a matter of compulsion. For that very reason, they held, the government should not attempt to do more than provide the basic necessities of social life.

In replacing the pursuit of individual happiness with the altruist standard of the common good, however, the new liberals took a more organic view of society. The individual had a duty to pursue the interests of his fellows and of society as a whole, and the duty could be enforced by the state as society's agent. Citing his view of the individual as a node in a network of social relationships, Montague wrote, "It follows that the interest of the citizen and the interest of the state are merely two names for the same thing. The State lives only in the life of the citizen, develops only in developing him. The true function of the State is to make the most of the citizen."[88] Herbert Asquith, the British prime minister whose administration passed the Old Age Pension and National Insurance Acts, said in an 1892 election address that "the collective action of the community may and ought to be employed positively ... to make the freedom of the individual a reality."[89] Roosevelt crowed in a message to Congress that under the New Deal there had been "an appeal from the clamor of many private and selfish interests . . . to the ideal of the public interest. Government became the representative and the trustee of the public interest."[90] In short, the universal and coercive institution of the state was now to reach much more deeply into the formerly private lives of citizens.

The classical liberals had held that while adults in a free society were capable of making their own decisions, initiating action, and taking responsibility for their lives, government aid that was provided automatically bred a corrupting sort of dependence, sapping the habit of independence. Observing the new trend in liberal thinking, Herbert Spencer complained that "habits of improvidence having for generations been cultivated by the Poor-Law, and the improvident enabled to multiply, the evils produced by compulsory charity are now proposed to be met by compulsory insurance."[91] But the new liberals had no confidence in the capacity of the ordinary person to conduct his own affairs rationally in any case, so there was nothing to lose by expanding government aid. In their eyes, they were simply replacing traditional and piecemeal forms of dependence with systematic and more rational ones.

Indeed, confidence in the rationality of government action was perhaps the most distinctive doctrine of the new liberals. Classical liberals had been suspicious of political power and of those who wield it. The *Federalist Papers*, for example, is a meditation on the danger of political power's being captured by factions—"special interests," to use the more contemporary term—and used for their own ends. The new liberals, by contrast, were confident that government bureaucrats were willing and able to achieve consensus in pursuit of public ends. The American liberals of the New Deal, as Cass Sunstein observes, assumed that public officials would be "independent, self-starting, technically expert, and apolitical agents of change." As a result, the New Dealers sought to expand the scope of action of public officials—by expanding the conception of rights to include economic goods, by setting up administrative agencies to escape the tripartite structure of government with its cumbersome "checks and balances," and by shifting power from state to federal government.[92] The way had been prepared for those political changes by a generation of thinkers who developed the concept of social engineering. John Dewey in particular was fond of the analogy that just as the physical sciences had given us control of nature, so the social sciences could now be used to control the organization of society for collective benefits—the state being the engineer in charge of the process.[93]

The net effect of those changes in the conception of society and state has been aptly summarized by Norman Barry:

> The birth of the modern theory of welfare depended on the reinterpretation of certain key political concepts: notably liberty, community and equality. The effect of this reinterpretation was to transform the nature of society from a conception of a loosely co-ordinating set of individuals bound together by common rules but lacking a common purpose, into a more intimate form of order (a *community*). If people were held together by social bonds that transcended contractual relationships then they could make claims on each other, as citizens of a common enterprise.... From this perspective, state welfare would cease to be regarded as an act of charity and would be seen as a form of entitlement.[94]

Welfare Rights

The idea that people have rights to certain goods provided by society was a natural consequence of the premises we have discussed, particularly the concept of positive freedom. After all, the concept of rights was classically conceived as a protection for individual liberty. When conceptions of liberty change, conceptions of rights can be expected to change with them. Three years after his "Four Freedoms" speech, FDR asked Congress to create a new bill of rights to underlie the welfare programs he had already created. "We have accepted, so to speak, a second Bill of Rights under which a new basis of security and prosperity can be secured for all—regardless of station, race or creed." Among the rights he wanted to include were the rights to "useful and remunerative" work, "adequate food and clothing and recreation," "adequate medical care," and "protection from the economic fear of old age, sickness, accident and unemployment."[95] The idea of adding such "rights" to the Constitution was not an afterthought on Roosevelt's part; it was something he had sought all along.[96]

As we saw in Chapter 2, Roosevelt's wish to create a constitutional right to welfare was never granted. But in America, as in other Western countries, the welfare state was associated with new rights at the other two levels we discussed: the statutory and the moral.

57

Welfare programs created new statutory rights, new entitlements, to government benefits; and the advocates of those programs often invoked a moral right to social support as a rationale for enacting them in the first place.

At one level, it is a tautology to observe that welfare programs created new statutory rights. The granting of benefits by a statute like Britain's National Insurance Act, or the Social Security Act in the United States, obviously creates a statutory right to those benefits. The same might be said of the original English Poor Law, enacted in 1601. But the nature and significance of such rights have changed over the last two centuries. As government has taken on new functions, it has changed its methods of operation. The public business of the state has been separated more clearly from the personal interests of rulers. Church and state have been put at arm's length. Political reforms have created a professional civil service, a bureaucracy that operates by fixed rules.

There is thus a vast distance between the Elizabethan Poor Law, which was administered in local parishes, by people who knew the recipients, and poverty programs in America today, which distribute billions of dollars each month in accordance with complicated formulas. The Poor Law was local and allowed for some discretion in distinguishing the deserving from the undeserving poor; current programs operate at the state and federal levels, and their conditions for eligibility have nothing to do with character. Pre-modern forms of government relief were continuous with private charity; modern poverty programs are categorically different. That difference was welcomed and deliberately promoted by the architects of the welfare state. The creation of statutory rights was intended to remove the "stigma" of receiving alms from others: that which can be claimed as a right does not depend on the grace of others or require gratitude to them.

The positive connotations of a right explain a curious reversal described by Himmelfarb. In the late 19th century, poor people who received private help from agencies such as the Charity Organization Society were held in higher esteem than those on the government dole: aid in the former case was given to those of good character whose need for help usually sprang from circumstances beyond their control. By contrast, "the opinion prevalent today [is] that charity is ignoble while state aid is honorable, reflected in the common view that it is demeaning for elderly parents to be dependent on their families but not demeaning to have them dependent on the state."[97] The explanation is that state aid is now regarded as a right, carrying with it the connotations of independence and citizenship. It was not so regarded a hundred years ago.

The notion that someone can be independent while being supported by the coercive transfer of wealth produced by others is the legacy of the intellectual sea change I have described. In England and America, countries with a strong individualist tradition, the advocates of the welfare state did not explicitly repudiate individualism, as the socialists did. They redefined it by redefining the concepts of freedom and rights but retaining their connotations of independence. As Stefan Collini said of Hobhouse, the new liberal "wanted to have his cake of Socialism and to eat it in accordance with Liberal principles."[98] A radical growth in government, and a radical change in the relationship between the individual and the state, was thus disguised by continuity in language and by the invocation of traditional individualist symbols such as bills of rights.

In implementation as well, the welfare state was often designed to minimize any sense of departure from tradition. The American Social Security system, for example, was deliberately designed to look like a private pension plan, with payroll taxes described as "contributions," despite the radical difference from any private plan: Social Security is compulsory, the pensions are not actually owned, the terms can be changed at any time by Congress, and the formulas relating benefits to taxes paid are skewed on behalf of lower income workers. As Rimlinger notes, the quasi-contractual form of the program "was a shrewd formula, for it covered the inevitable element of social compulsion with a veneer of individualism."[99]

Conclusion

The modern welfare state emerged over the course of 50 years, from the 1880s to the 1930s. The programs introduced by the Prussian autocrat Otto von Bismarck were adopted and modified in England and America by a new generation of liberals who sought to cloak the expansion of government in the familiar garb of individualism. The welfare state was not an inevitable response to developments in industrial capitalism. It was a response to certain problems as interpreted by a new philosophical outlook that captured the allegiance of social thinkers and activists.

One such problem was the continuing existence of poverty in the context of rising wealth for the vast majority of people. Such poverty elicited sympathy from the new middle class and an outpouring of philanthropy. But that sympathy was transformed by the altruist element of the new philosophy into a duty that could be enforced by the state. At the same time, the premise of environmental determinism undermined the distinction between the deserving and the undeserving poor, a distinction that had led earlier generations to oppose any level of government relief beyond a bare minimum.

The other major problem was the new forms of economic risk faced by working people in a complex market economy. Once again, the problem was being addressed by private forms of insurance and mutual aid. It was only the premises of the new philosophy that transformed the existence of economic risk into an argument for government programs. The concepts of positive freedom and economic coercion were invoked to argue that workers who lost their jobs were victims of social forces and had the right to redress in the form of social benefits. Imbued with the belief in economic determinism, reformers did not trust working people to act responsibly. As altruists, moreover, they were unwilling to let the irresponsible suffer the consequences.

At the same time, the new philosophy embraced a collectivist view of society as an entity or organism transcending individuals and the myriad private, self-interested relationships among them. The advocates of this philosophy had a powerful confidence in the benevolence and rationality of government action. As a result, they believed that government can and should supersede the efforts of private individuals to address the problems of poverty and economic risk.

In short, the welfare state is a set of institutions that emerged at a specific point in history, the response to a particular situation by thinkers and activists operating on a particular set of assumptions. There was nothing inevitable about it. If the intellectual changes described in this chapter had never occurred, there is no reason to think we would have a welfare state today. Consequently, there is no reason to assume that it will be a permanent part of the social landscape. To determine whether the welfare state does or should have a future, we must now examine critically the assumption that people have a right to its services. Having examined the legal character of welfare rights, and the circumstances under which the concept of such rights arose, we must now ask whether the concept can be *justified*. Is it a valid concept? In the following chapters, we shall examine the moral, political, and economic arguments, pro and con.

4. Economic Freedom and Economic Risk

The welfare state was advanced as the means to address two different problems: poverty and economic risk. It involves two different types of programs for different constituencies: poverty programs for the poor and social insurance for the working and middle classes. Underlying those differences, however, is a common legal and moral basis. The welfare state by its nature creates legal rights to goods. Although the American courts have never recognized a constitutional right to welfare, the rationale for the welfare state assumes the existence of a moral right to public provision. It is time to consider the validity of that assumption. What moral responsibility do citizens have toward their fellow citizens? What sort of aid, if any, are people morally entitled to expect from the state? Do people have *rights* to the public provision of food, shelter, medical care, pensions, and other such goods?

If the concept of welfare rights can be justified in moral terms, if people really do have rights to such goods, then we must keep the welfare state in something like its present form. A civilized society cannot disregard a genuine human right. We may attempt piecemeal reforms to slow the growth in the cost of welfare programs, and to ameliorate the perverse incentives for irresponsibility they create, but we cannot eliminate the programs per se. If the concept of a welfare right is *not* valid, however, then people are not morally entitled to expect society to provide for them. Lacking a moral justification, the welfare state is nothing more than a mechanism for transferring wealth from those who earned it to those who did not. It is a system of injustice, backed only by tradition and the coercive power of the state, and we must look for ways to wind it down.

It is important to distinguish rights from expectations. The enjoyment of a good, or the awareness that others enjoy it, or sometimes even the awareness that it exists, can easily give rise to the feeling that we ought to have it and that life without it is subnormal. Workers become attached to their wages and benefits as something more

63

than contractual provisions; paid vacations, maternity leave, health insurance, and the like come to be viewed as inalienable rights. When a life-saving drug or medical procedure is first introduced, universal access to it is quickly elevated into a right.

That expectations can create a spirit of entitlement is a politically significant fact. The public judges politicians by whether they can "deliver the goods." Beneficiaries of government transfer programs are outraged at the prospect of cuts in the benefits to which they have become accustomed. In moral terms, however, an expectation is not necessarily a right. That depends on whether it is rational or not, whether it is based on wishes or on facts, whether it can be supported by a valid ethical rationale. We are speaking here of basic human or moral rights, which set the fundamental terms on which people can live together in society. Rights in this sense are the enduring principles by which society is organized, not the constantly changing expectations that arise from economic and technological progress.

What, then, is the case for welfare rights? And what is the case against them? We can distill the essential issues and arguments from the foregoing legal and historical analysis, as well as from contemporary discussions. Advocates of welfare rights have offered three fundamental lines of argument for their position:

- *The argument from economic freedom*: The function of rights is to protect our freedom to act, but what good is political freedom if we are not also free from hunger and the risks of unemployment, illness, and old age? We must have a right to protection against those economic risks to our security.
- *The argument from benevolence*: When someone is in need, compassion requires us to help if we can; this moral obligation entails a right on the part of the needy.
- *The argument from community*: We form a single society, and part of the social contract is that we will take care of each other when the need arises. People have a right to expect that if they play by the rules, they will not be left behind; and those who succeed by the grace of society have an obligation to help.

Each of those arguments deserves its own analysis. We will see that none of them is valid, none can provide a good reason for believing in a moral right to welfare benefits. Indeed, we will see that each of them, on closer analysis, shows that welfare rights are incompatible with the genuine rights that individuals possess and the genuine values that a free society has to offer. We will begin in this chapter with the issue of economic freedom.

The Concept of Freedom

The classical rights to life, liberty, and property, as we saw in Chapter 2, are rights to freedom of action. The right to life, for example, is not a guarantee that I will succeed in the attempt to preserve myself; it is a guarantee that no one will assault or murder me, or otherwise interfere coercively with my attempt to live. The right to property is not a guarantee that I will actually acquire goods; it is a guarantee that no one will steal the things I have acquired, or interfere with the processes of work and voluntary exchange by which I seek to acquire them. By contrast, welfare rights are rights to have certain goods regardless of whether I actually earn them. The classical rights of liberty protect one's *freedom from* coercive interference by others; welfare rights protect *freedom to* possess and enjoy certain goods. Liberty rights are concerned with the *processes* by which we act and interact; welfare rights are concerned with the *outcomes* of such actions.

The core rationale for rights to goods is the concept of positive freedom. Without the enjoyment of certain goods, it is argued, individuals cannot achieve the ends that freedom is for. They are not truly free if they are starving, if they lack shelter, if they cannot get treatment for illness. What good is the legal freedom to act if we lack the basic necessities of life? In short, real freedom is something positive, not negative. Real freedom is not merely the absence of restraint; it requires the real opportunity, the real capacity, to obtain the things we need.

From Thomas Hill Green to Franklin Delano Roosevelt, that argument was a staple in the liberal case for the welfare state, and it continues to play that role. "The social welfare state," argue Norman Furniss and Timothy Tilton, "aspires to free classes of citizens from the pressure of external circumstances, class handicaps, and economic insecurity through the more equal distribution of economic and political resources."[1] In a 1969 federal welfare case, Judge Walter Mansfield argued that while "receipt of welfare benefits may not at the present time constitute the exercise of a constitutional right," the

65

Preamble of the Constitution implies certain standards "of humanity and decency. One of these . . . is the desire to ensure that indigent, unemployable citizens will have the bare minimums required for existence, without which our expressed fundamental constitutional rights and liberties frequently cannot be exercised and therefore become meaningless."[2] At the symbolic level, the fact that food stamp booklets carry the insignia of the Liberty Bell is doubtless a reflection of the same reasoning. "Necessitous men are not free," said President Roosevelt.[3]

That extension of the classical concept of liberty may have a superficial plausibility. Beneath the surface, however, it is invalid. The concept of positive freedom refers to something fundamentally different from—and incompatible with—freedom in the ordinary sense.

Reality and Freedom

The concept of freedom refers to a condition in which a person can act independently, choosing among a range of alternative actions. Conversely, the concept of coercion refers to a condition in which other people have deprived one of the capacity to act independently. Freedom is a value in human life because we need this capacity. Human beings are not automatons. We have the power of reason, which includes the ability to think in terms of abstract principles, to assimilate large masses of information, to weigh evidence for and against a given conclusion, to adopt long-range goals, to project the consequences of our actions into the future, and to deliberate among alternative courses of action. We need the freedom to act on the basis of our own judgment in choosing both the ends we seek and the means by which we pursue them.

In regard to the ends, human beings have a range of needs that must be satisfied—not just physical needs like food and shelter but psychological, spiritual, and social needs as well. But those needs can be fulfilled in countless different ways. Any number of jobs, for example, can satisfy our needs for economic support, intellectual challenge, and social interaction, in different ways and to different degrees. No two individuals are identical, and the individual is in the best position to determine which of the myriad goals, ways of life, and long-term projects available to him will best suit his particular needs. In allocating time and energy to our goals, we constantly face choices between rival values. We face "trade-offs," as economists call them: work vs. family, income vs. leisure, security vs. risk, and the like. The freedom to make these choices is a fundamental part of independent action.

Of equal importance is freedom in choosing *how* to achieve the things we want. He who wills the end must also will the means, but the means one could employ in pursuit of a given end are as diverse as the ends themselves. Even an impoverished inner-city youth looking for his first job has choices to make: where in the city will he conduct his search? which people will he ask for leads? is it more efficient to use the "Help Wanted" section of the paper or to canvass the neighborhood merchants? One's choice about how to get things done depends on the particular information at one's disposal, as well as one's abilities, preferences, convictions, and loyalties. No two people are alike in all those respects.

Both the ends and the means of action typically involve other people, and independent action therefore includes the freedom to choose the people with whom one associates. The value of such freedom is obvious in personal affairs: who could imagine giving up the freedom to choose his own friends? But it is also important in economic relationships. In dealing with each other as employers and employees, buyers and sellers, and the like, we need the freedom to set the terms on which we are willing to trade. Since almost everything we do involves some interaction with people, we cannot have the freedom to pursue our goals unless we have the freedom to decide whether and how we wish to deal with others. That freedom serves not only to help us find those people with whom we can best cooperate to achieve our goals but also to help us avoid those people who pose a threat or whose actions or character we disapprove of. Indeed, moral judgment is one of the ways in which we hold other people accountable for their actions. In our personal lives, we take for granted the freedom to steer clear of unreliable friends. The same freedom makes it possible for employers (unless contractually forbidden) to fire workers who abuse drugs or alcohol, fail to perform their jobs, or harass other employees. That freedom makes it possible for employees to quit if they are treated unfairly, and for customers to shop elsewhere when the price is too high or the courtesy too low.

Such are the basic dimensions of liberty in the classical sense. Freedom always involves the capacity to choose among a range of alternative actions. In that sense, freedom is a positive concept. But it is also a negative concept: the freedom to choose exists as long as no one interferes with the choice coercively, using force to prevent the person from selecting one of the alternatives. In any case, there is a difference between the question of which particular alternatives a person has available and the question of whether he is free to choose among them. "Whether or not I am my own master and can follow my own choice and whether the possibilities from which I must choose are many or few," wrote F. A. Hayek, "are two entirely different questions."[4] The first of those questions is the real issue of freedom; the second is an issue of my efficacy or power. Two people can differ markedly in the opportunities they have before them and yet be equally free from interference by others in choosing among their respective opportunities. A diner at Joe's Cafe has a more limited menu to choose from than does a diner at the Four Seasons, but both people are equally free to choose among the entrees available. The fact that Joe's does not serve oysters on the half shell is not an issue of freedom.

To be sure, there is not always a hard and fast distinction between the number of alternatives one has and the degree of one's freedom to choose among them. Theoretically, any obstacle, restraint, or limitation may be looked at in either of two ways: we may view it (1) as something that *eliminates* one or more alternatives a person would otherwise have available or (2) as something that *prevents* the person from choosing one or more of those alternatives. The difference lies in whether we consider the limitation as affecting the range of alternatives he has or the process of choosing among them. Advocates of positive freedom have exploited this fact, insisting that lack of a certain opportunity because of poverty, illness, or disability deprives a person of the freedom to choose that opportunity. Conversely, we could in principle view overt coercion, physical force, or violence, not as something that prevents a person from choosing an alternative but as something that simply removes certain alternatives he would otherwise have.[5]

Nevertheless, there are real differences between (1) and (2). One difference is whether the obstacle or limitation is imposed by reality or by other people. When some fact of reality affects the range of alternatives we face, it is wishful thinking to regard it as an obstacle to what we would otherwise be free to do. Facts are facts. The world operates a certain way, according to causal laws, and the constraints imposed by nature are the foundation for human choice, not a barrier to it. A farmer plants a field and tends it over the growing season, but a hailstorm destroys the crop before he can harvest it. It would be bizarre to say that the hailstorm abridged his freedom to reap what he has sown. As a natural event, the hailstorm is a misfortune that eliminates the possibility of a harvest. By contrast, if a government price-support regulation forbids the farmer to harvest the crop, the restraint arises from human action and does abridge his freedom to do what he otherwise could.

Similarly, if I cannot run a five-minute mile, my incapacity does not abridge my freedom to do so; it is simply a fact about my nature. But if I *can* run that fast, and someone forces me to wear lead weights as a handicap, he is restricting my freedom. The concept of freedom distinguishes man-made limitations from natural ones, such as the external constraint of the hailstorm and the constraints set by our own capacities. But even if a limitation does arise from the actions of another person, it may not be an issue of freedom. A man asks the woman he loves to marry him, but the feeling isn't mutual and she turns him down. Does her indifference limit his freedom? Surely not: without her consent, marrying her is simply not an alternative for him. If the feeling *is* mutual, however, and the marriage is blocked by the parents' opposition, then the lovers are not free to do what their own consent made possible. In general, there is a difference between the negative "act" of failing to provide someone with a benefit or opportunity and the positive act of depriving him of it. Absent his beloved's consent, marrying her is not an action on the suitor's list of alternatives, and her refusal to put it on his list is not equivalent to the act of a third party who prevents him from choosing that alternative.

The concept of positive freedom arises from an invalid attempt to ignore the distinctions we have just drawn by insisting that the presence of certain options among one's alternatives is equivalent to freedom of choice among one's alternatives and that the absence of an option is equivalent to coercive interference with one's freedom. If we broaden the concept of freedom in this way, we empty it of meaning. We already have concepts to designate the range of alternative actions one has available—the concepts of "power," "ability," and "opportunity," among others. We do not need another name for the same thing. If human beings lacked choice, if our actions were governed by causal factors in the way that the actions of a rock or a tree are, we would not need the concept of freedom. We would simply describe our actions in terms of what we can and cannot do. That's how we describe the behavior of rocks and trees. But we do have choice, and we need a term to designate the unimpeded exercise of choice. That term is "freedom."

Its antonym, "coercion," also has a specific meaning. If we think of freedom as measured by the range of alternative actions we have, then any factor that diminishes the range from what it might otherwise have been must be considered coercive. The concept of "coercion" would then include not only the use of force but also such things as high interest rates, which can prevent me from buying a house, and the Earth's gravitational field, which prevents me from walking on air. "Coercion" would then refer to any causal factor whatever, and the term would have no meaning apart from causality. What if we restrict the term to the actions of other people? That is a step in the right direction, but not far enough; we need to go on to distinguish between the negative act of not providing a benefit and the positive action of harming another. Otherwise we have the bizarre implication that each of us is engaged at every moment in the constant use of coercion against every other human being whom we do not, in that moment, wish to speak to, trade with, or enjoy the company of.

The concepts of freedom and coercion are restricted to human action because of the central, distinctive feature of such action: the power to choose. Choice is the selection of an action from a range of alternatives on the basis of deliberation. We need to deliberate in order to choose what goals to pursue, taking account of the needs that reality imposes, and to choose what means to employ, taking account of the information we acquire about reality. That is the human mode of life. Anything that prevents us from acting as we choose, on the basis of our deliberation, is a fundamental threat to that mode of life. If we did not use the terms "freedom" and "coercion" to identify the absence or presence of such a threat, we would simply need to make up other terms in their place. As the foregoing makes clear, however, there's no need to undertake that semantic task. Freedom is the condition in which we can act independently, and the essence of independence is the power to act on the basis of our own deliberate judgment. Coercion is the condition in which other people have deprived us of the capacity to act independently, and they do so only through some positive action that forces us to comply with their will rather than our own.

Positive Freedom versus Real Freedom

A law professor writing on health care policy offers a particularly egregious example of the errors we have just discussed. Attacking the view that the core issue of liberty is protection against intrusions by the state, she argues that

> disease, injury, and threats to health constrain freedom with-
> out the help of any state, although states can surely exacer-
> bate such dangers. . . . Any hypothetical state of nature
> would have to include dangers and threats to liberty posed
> by the inevitability of disease.[6]

Precisely because disease is an inevitable feature of human life, however, it is not a limitation on freedom. This extension of the concept of freedom implies that the existence of disease-causing microbes, and of injury-causing forces such as gravity, violates the individual's freedom of choice—a notion that makes sense only if we assume that individuals in some sense "ought" to be able to choose their fates in complete disregard of the facts.

A slightly less bizarre invocation of the same concept is the argu-ment that since freedom means autonomy, it must include the capac-ity to adopt whatever mode of life one chooses—regardless of any other consideration. In the extreme case, freedom is said to require independence from any sort of economic necessity, including the need to work for a living. In a market economy, one philosopher asserts, people are deprived of the right to be idle:

> [P]aid employment is the would-be idler's only genuine
> option. . . . It is therefore fair to say that would-be idlers
> without independent means are involuntarily employed; that
> they are economically coerced into entering the labor market.
> To the degree that they are, withholding [government] bene-
> fits from them would be objectionable in the way, though
> perhaps not to the degree, that conscripting them directly
> into the workforce would be.[7]

Here we have the spectacle of philosophy in denial. What the author is demanding is not freedom in any meaningful sense but

71

the chance to live without responsibility. The need to produce if one wishes to consume is not an arbitrary human convention, a form of conscription imposed on those who prefer idleness. From the simplest food and garments to color TVs and heart-transplant technology, goods are produced by human thought and effort. They do not exist in nature, ready-made; they result from discovery, invention, investment, and the transformation of raw materials by human action. In a complex society, of course, it is possible to acquire goods without work, through voluntary gift or coercive transfer. But the failure to confer such a benefit on the would-be idler is not the same as a coercive interference with his freedom to choose idleness. The only actual victims of coercion in the author's scenario are the productive people who would be forced to pay—those who would be conscripted through the tax system to work for the idler.

Welfare policy provides a clear illustration of the difference between genuine coercion, which involves a positive, deliberate harm or threat of harm, and the failure to provide a benefit. Proposals to cut welfare programs are typically greeted with the accusation that cuts would harm the beneficiaries of the program. Rep. John Lewis (D-Ga.) recently described a welfare reform bill as an "onslaught on children, poor people, and the disabled, reminiscent of Nazi Germany."[8] The analogy with Nazi Germany is telling—and not merely for its lack of any sense of proportion. No one is proposing that children, poor people, or the disabled be killed, or put in concentration camps, or expelled from the country, or in any other way harmed by government aggression. The issue is how much positive help they should be given, and a decrease in the level of help is not an act of coercion, despite the fact that it may disappoint the expectations of welfare recipients.

For example, one popular welfare reform measure is to end the policy of automatically increasing monthly payments to a mother on welfare when she has another child. Poverty lawyers have challenged the measure in court, arguing that it is a government intrusion into the mothers' freedom of choice about bearing children. But in fact the reform simply makes women on welfare subject to the same "obstacles"—the same facts of reality—that women not on welfare face, whose income does not automatically increase with the number of children they bear. This is a distinction that the Supreme Court has drawn repeatedly in cases brought by welfare rights advocates.

In *Harris v. McRae,* for example, it held that Congress could forbid Medicaid funds from being used to pay for abortions; though the freedom to have an abortion was protected under the law, the government does not violate that freedom by deciding not to fund its exercise:

> It simply does not follow that a woman's freedom of choice carries with it a constitutional entitlement to the financial resources to avail herself of the full range of protected choices. . . . Although government may not place obstacles in the path of a woman's exercise of her freedom of choice, it need not remove those not of its own creation. Indigency falls in the latter category.[9]

What if someone does want to support himself by work but has few choices? Suppose an employer offers me a job with onerous conditions attached, like poor wages or a dangerous working environment. Exponents of positive freedom say that I am forced to accept the conditions, since I need work. "If I have no option but to starve or to accept a lousy job," argues Philippe van Parijs, "I am not really free to turn the latter down."[10] But the fact is that I could refuse the job. The employer is not putting a gun to my head. If I do refuse, I am no worse off than if the employer had had no job to offer in the first place. If he is violating my freedom by not offering a job with higher pay, would he violate my freedom by offering no job at all? Is my next-door neighbor violating my freedom by not offering me work?

Consider John Kenneth Galbraith's comparison of work and slavery:

> The worker in a Calcutta jute mill who loses his job—like his American counterpart during the Great Depression—has no high prospect of ever finding another. He has no savings. Nor does he have unemployment insurance. The alternative to his present employment, accordingly, is slow but definitive starvation. So though nominally a free worker, he is compelled. The fate of a defecting southern slave before the Civil War or a serf before Alexander II was not appreciably more painful. The choice between hunger and flogging may well be a matter of taste.[11]

Galbraith's jute mill workers are not unfree merely because they must work in order to eat. That necessity is not a punishment imposed by the arbitrary will of the factory owner, as is a flogging administered by a slaveholder. The factory job gives the worker a way to meet a need imposed by nature, an option that he would not otherwise have had. The factory owner who fires a worker is not positively harming the latter but is withdrawing a benefit. That is categorically different from the slave owner who uses coercion— the threat of positive harm like a whipping—to compel obedience. If the worker goes hungry after losing his job, the hunger is not a lashing imposed on him by the owner; it is a natural consequence of the fact that the worker is no longer producing.[12]

In the same way, the inventor of a new life-saving device may offer it only for a price that I cannot afford. Does that violate my freedom to live? No. He has not actually done anything to me, and I am no worse off than if he had not invented the device. Fifty years ago, people whose kidneys were failing needed dialysis every bit as much as they do today, but there were no dialysis machines. Was that condition a violation of their freedom from kidney failure? Was Mother Nature violating their rights by making their kidneys fail without a remedy? Were the scientists and engineers who had failed to invent dialysis machines violating their rights? It makes no sense, as we have seen, to claim that one's freedom is abridged by the natural process of disease. Nor does it make sense to claim that someone who could forestall the process violates my freedom by failing to do so on terms I can accept.

Those who defend the concept of positive freedom, finally, almost never employ the concept consistently. If economic pressures and constraints count as instances of coercion, the "victims" are not limited to workers at the bottom of the economic ladder and other natural objects of sympathy. A best-selling author who leaves one giant publishing conglomerate to accept a better offer with another has diminished the freedom of the first. The struggling inhabitants of a small town who flock to the new Wal-Mart in an effort to stretch their budgets are using force against the local retailers they abandon. The Ford Motor Company was the victim of a massive loss of freedom when customers refused to buy the Edsel. If the concept of economic freedom had any validity, it would apply in those cases no less than in the others we have discussed.

In any case, the concept runs up against two stubborn facts. The first is that we cannot meaningfully speak of being free from the constraints set by reality, including the fact that we need to produce in order to have any goods. The second is that when we cooperate with others in the course of making a living—as buyers and sellers, employers and workers, even as donors and recipients of charity— the absence of a benefit is not the same as a positive harm. Another person's choice not to employ me, not to buy my wares, or not to give me charity is not a violation of my freedom or an exercise of coercion (unless we have an antecedent contract). It leaves me where I was before—no worse off, and certainly not less independent.

If someone lacks the goods or opportunities that fall within some conception of positive freedom, moreover, the only way his "free- dom" can be preserved is by forcing others to supply what he lacks. Reality cannot be forced; the need to produce a good before it is consumed cannot be legislated out of existence. Goods can only be redistributed from one person to another. The government may provide the goods directly, through cash or in-kind programs paid for by taxes, thus forcing taxpayers to spend their money on grants to others. Or it may issue regulations dictating the terms on which jobs are offered, goods are sold, contracts are written, and so on. Either way, the price of positive freedom is the sacrifice of genu- ine liberty.

These bedrock truths are easily lost sight of in the complexity of an industrial—and now an information—economy. People do not live as self-sufficient farmers, facing nature directly and producing everything they consume. They work in specialized jobs, often in large corporations, and buy the things they wish to consume. The choices of millions of people, interacting in the marketplace, deter- mine what jobs, retail goods, and commercial opportunities will be available—and at what prices and on what terms.

The more specialized one's role in the division of labor, and the larger the market in which one operates, the more subject one becomes to distant and impersonal changes in consumer demand, changes in supply by competitors, and financial factors affecting the value of the currency and the business cycle. We have seen that a major impetus for the concept of welfare rights during the course of the 19th century was the phenomenon of economic risk that arises from such dependence on the market. How is independence possible without protection against those forces? It was the desire for protec- tion against economic risk, as well as the risk of job loss through illness or old age, that led to the creation of social insurance programs such as Medicare, unemployment insurance, and Social Security, as well as poverty programs.

In the end, however, such complexity does not change the basic reality of production and trade. The risks that arise from the economic flow of supply and demand are not the results of anyone's intention. As F. A. Hayek often observed, they are the results of human action but not of human design. They result from millions of people choosing whether or not to confer benefits on each other, their choices summed by the laws of mathematics. In that sense, economic risks are natural risks, since they arise from economic laws that are not man-made.

An auto worker loses his job. What is the cause? Perhaps the company misread consumer tastes and its cars are not selling well. Perhaps improvements in the assembly line make the worker's job unnecessary. Perhaps foreign companies have been producing competitive makes of cars at lower cost. Whatever the case, has the worker literally been forced off the job, or suffered a loss of freedom? Certainly his opportunities have been affected for the worse if he must now accept a lower paying job. But no third party is actually preventing his former employer from keeping him on. The auto company chose not to continue exchanging its wage for his labor. It did so, moreover, because its customers chose not to continue exchanging their money for its cars, or because capital goods producers chose to make new labor-saving technology available at a price the company could afford. The entire situation reduces to the actions of individuals choosing to engage or not to engage in trade, as an exercise of their economic freedom.

Like natural risks, economic risks can be dealt with by insurance. But genuine insurance, like any other good, is a value that has to be produced. It can't be legislated into existence. When the state offers a form of insurance to those who cannot or will not pay for it themselves, it must force others to supply it, through taxes or through regulation, sacrificing genuine liberty in the process. As we will see presently, for example, government efforts to make health insurance more widely available involve a straightforward coercive transfer from some people to others.

The concept of positive freedom, therefore, is misconceived and cannot support the notion of welfare rights. The concept ignores the distinction between natural and man-made constraints on action. It ignores the distinction between failing to offer someone a benefit and imposing an actual harm. And the pursuit of positive freedom through state action violates genuine liberty. Someone who claims a right to a good that he has not produced (or acquired by some other voluntary means) is doing one of two things: either he is claiming a right to have nature supply him with goods without effort, which is absurd; or he is claiming a right to take goods from others against their will, which is unjust.

The Destruction of Freedom

These philosophical issues have real consequences. The attempt to promote positive freedom through government action has led to the sacrifice of genuine freedom—and the loss of real opportunities—across a broad front. An examination of two areas in particular, poverty programs and health care policy, will illustrate the scope of the destruction.

Freedom, Poverty, and Opportunity

As Charles Murray observes, the rationale for the vast expansion of welfare spending during the 1960s was the belief that poverty had structural causes outside the individual's control:

> What emerged in the mid-1960s was an almost unbroken intellectual consensus that the individualist explanation of poverty was altogether outmoded and reactionary. Poverty . . . was produced by conditions that had nothing to do with individual effort or virtue. *Poverty was not the fault of the individual but of the system.*[13]

That consensus was an extreme form of the environmental determinism that, as we saw in the last chapter, was a key tenet of the 19th-century advocates of the welfare state. And the consensus is wrong now, as it was then.

To begin with, poverty is not a fixed condition. The poverty rate as reported by the Census Bureau has been more or less flat at 13 to 15 percent of the population since the 1970s—about 40 million people at present. That figure gives us a snapshot of how many people are poor at a given moment in time, but it does not show movement into and out of poverty. In fact, there is a good deal of movement, as researchers at the Census Bureau found in a special study tracking individuals during the years 1990–91. About 45 million people had incomes below the poverty level for at least two months during 1990; 48.5 million did in 1991. But most of those spells of poverty were short: the median spell was four months, and only 18 percent were a year or longer, reflecting the common experience of short-term income declines between jobs, during off-seasons, or after a divorce. Only half of those people, about 24 million, had *annual* incomes below the poverty line in 1990, and more than 20 percent of that group, over 5 million, had risen out of poverty in the following year. Only 10.6 million were poor for all 24 months of the study period.[14]

What determines movements into and out of poverty and holds back those who are poor for long stretches? Obviously, not many people actually choose to be poor. That is one reason for the common view that poverty is the fault of the system, and for the reluctance to "blame the victims" by holding them responsible for their condition. But relatively few poor people are pure victims of circumstance, either. They may not choose poverty directly, but they do make choices that have long-term economic consequences. Three factors in particular are strongly associated with poverty: education, marital status, and employment.[15] The chance of living in poverty is directly related to the level of education one has attained. Women who are single parents, along with their children, are much more likely to be poor than are married couples and their families. And of course those who work are much less likely to be poor than are those who don't.

These factors obviously combine and reinforce each other. Many single mothers, for example, are teenagers who have dropped out of school and are not working. In an exhaustive study of traits associated with the "underclass," the long-term poor, M. Anne Hill and June O'Neill found that teenage girls who are dependent on welfare are three times more likely to be high school dropouts than are teenage girls in the general population (45 percent versus 15 percent). Of teenage boys with low workforce attachment (as measured by their employment histories), 37 percent were high school dropouts, versus 16 percent in the general youth population.[16]

It is also clear that none of these factors—education, family structure, or employment—is entirely outside the control of the individuals concerned. Education is perhaps the most obvious case. As Table

TABLE 4.1
EDUCATION AND POVERTY

Education	Poverty Rate (percentage)
Did not complete high school	25.6
High school degree, no college	10.4
High school degree, some college	7.0
College (bachelor's) degree or higher	3.0

4.1 indicates, high school dropouts have a much higher poverty rate than do those who stay the course.[17] Some young people doubtless leave high school early because of economic necessity—for example, the need to replace the income of a departed or disabled parent. (If they do enter the workforce and stay in it, they will almost certainly rise above the poverty level quickly; as noted below, poverty is rare among full-time workers.) More often, however, dropping out is a function of values and preferences, of boredom in class and the lure of the streets. Of the teenage boys in Hill and O'Neill's study, 19 percent had spent time in jail (versus 4 percent of all teenage boys), one of many indications that their lack of education, and the poverty they could expect as a result, was produced by behavioral problems rather than external economic forces.[18]

The same is true for family status. Of all the people living in families headed by a married couple, the percentage who live below the poverty level was 6.8 percent in 1995. For those living in single-mother households, the percentage was 36.5 percent.[19] Indeed, the factor overwhelmingly responsible for entering the welfare system is becoming a single mother, either through divorce or by having a child out of wedlock. That factor alone accounts for about 75 percent of new entries on the welfare rolls. As Mary Jo Bane and David Ellwood observed, "If we could prevent the formation of new single-parent families, we could largely eliminate the need for AFDC."[20] Reliance on welfare is particularly high among unwed teenage mothers, 77 percent of whom are on the rolls within five years of their first child's birth.[21] No one and nothing is forcing those young women to have babies; the narrowing of their opportunities in life is the product of their own choices. The situation of divorced mothers is more complicated: they do not control the behavior of their spouses, and the government does not enforce very well the child-support payments to which they are entitled by the marital contract. Yet it was their decision to get married in the first place and to bear children; and the possibility of divorce is a foreseeable risk attached to those decisions.

Of the three major factors, work is the most important, and it is the most reliable means of escaping poverty. In 1995 only 2.7 percent of those who worked full-time during the year were living below the poverty level. But lack of work is also the factor most often invoked in the argument from economic freedom. Unemployment has often been seen as a structural problem in the economy, driven by forces far outside the individual's control. William Julius Wilson, for example, claims that a primary cause of poverty is loss of jobs in the inner cities. Most of the poor, he argues, would like to work, but the jobs have fled to the suburbs, leaving inner-city people trapped in poverty.[22] That is undoubtedly true of some people. Yet here, too, the numbers suggest that individuals have a large measure of control. In 1995, according to the Bureau of Labor Statistics, some 5.7 million persons who were not in the workforce said they wanted a job, but nearly 60 percent of them had not searched for a job in the past year. Of the 2.4 million who did search for work but gave up, only 400,000 said they were discouraged about their prospects.[23] Even a majority of nonworking black youth in the inner cities thought it would be easy to find a minimum wage job.[24]

The claim that most of the poor are locked into their poverty by social forces is also belied by measures of long-term economic mobility. Mobility is measured by the way individuals change their position in the overall distribution of income, from the bottom of the economic ladder to the top. That distribution is often reported in terms of classes: the lowest 20 percent received X amount of national income in one year and Y amount in another year. But the same individuals do not make up the lowest 20 percent of the population from one year to the next. To understand mobility, we must follow real individuals across time. Table 4.2 summarizes data compiled by the Institute for Social Research at the University of Michigan, which followed income earners from 1975 to 1991.[25] Each row in the table tells us what happened to those who started out in a given part of the income distribution in 1975. Of those who began in the lowest quintile, only 5.1 percent remained there. The other

TABLE 4.2
ECONOMIC MOBILITY

Income Quintile, 1975	Percentage in Quintile, 1991				
	1st	2nd	3rd	4th	5th
1st	5.1	14.6	21.0	30.3	29.0
2nd	4.2	23.5	20.3	25.2	26.8
3rd	3.3	19.3	28.3	30.1	19.0
4th	1.9	9.3	18.8	32.6	37.4
5th	0.9	2.8	10.2	23.6	62.5

95 percent had increased their income enough to place them in higher brackets, and nearly a third (29 percent) had made it to the top. Of those who began in the top bracket, over 60 percent remained there; the rest moved down in the distribution, a handful (0.9 percent) all the way to the bottom. The overall pattern, which is consistent with other studies,[26] shows a high degree of mobility, and thus of individual efficacy. This is not the picture of a caste society, with people rigidly locked in their "places."

People across the entire income spectrum in 1975 improved their economic position. The average income gain between 1975 and 1991 by individuals who started in the 1st (lowest) quintile in 1975 was $25,322. The average gain by those starting in the 5th quintile was $3,974 (all figures are in 1993 dollars). The rich did get richer over this period, but the poor got a lot richer. Meanwhile, young people, immigrants, and others joining the labor force—people who were not earning income in 1975—took the place of those who had left the bottom quintile and began the process by which they, too, would move up in time.

There is, however, one clear and unambiguous way in which the poor are victims of coercion. Government regulation of the economy, backed by the force of law, affects the poor in myriad ways that restrict their freedom, preventing them from taking advantage of opportunities made available by their circumstances and their own efforts. The most important of these restraints are the ones that prevent the poor from working.

Minimum wage laws were ostensibly introduced to protect workers' right to a "decent wage." Increasing the price of unskilled labor, however, diminishes the amount that employers demand: they will not employ those who produce less value than the wage, and such people are deprived of the opportunity to work at all. The old rule of thumb was that a 10 percent increase in the minimum wage caused a 1 to 3 percent decrease in teenage employment. The minimum wage, however, is only one of the many restrictions that government places on employment. Others include regulations on hours worked, overtime pay, and other working conditions; and mandatory fringe benefits such as family leave and health insurance. All of those add to the effective cost of hiring a person. "For a typical small business," according to Michael Tanner, "the total tax and regulatory burden for hiring an additional worker is more than $5,400. At best, that is $5,400 that is not going to the worker. At worst, the cost prevents the hiring of the worker."[27]

Moreover, hundreds of occupations are licensed at the state and local level, which restricts the number of people who can work in them. There is no evidence that occupational licensure in general protects the public from unqualified practitioners, and there is abundant evidence that it serves primarily to enrich existing practitioners by limiting competition.[28] That is particularly true of the kind of jobs most likely to be available to the poor. For example, many cities and states require those who braid hair, a popular service in black neighborhoods, to obtain a cosmetology license, often requiring 2,000 or more hours of training, none of which has anything to do with braiding. The government puts comparable obstacles in the way of starting the kind of small businesses that might be possible for a poor person to undertake, such as taxi and van services, pushcart food vending, catering, home-based day care, newsstands, and trash removal. New York City, for example, restricts the number of yellow taxis (the only kind allowed to pick up passengers on the street) so severely that the price of a cab medallion is far beyond the means of most self-employed drivers. New York also bans private van services that might compete with the public buses. It allows only 4,000 licenses for food vendors in the street and 1,700 for sidewalk merchandise vendors.[29] Even when governments do not put such overt limits on the number of businesses, they create a chilling effect by requiring applications and hearings, by delaying approvals, and by demanding complex paperwork.

The theorists who viewed the poor as locked into poverty by social forces beyond their control tended to view poverty programs as compensation for deprivations the poor suffered at the hands of the market. "The central question of entitlement during the mid-1960s," wrote Neil Gilbert, "focused not so much on the worthiness of potential welfare recipients as on the range of benefits that they deserved. . . . According to the conventional wisdom of that era, the poor were the innocent casualties of capitalism and were therefore entitled to be compensated for its failures."[30] In fact, however, the poor have been beneficiaries of capitalism. As we have seen, they have enjoyed a vast improvement in opportunities and standards of living as a result of technological and economic growth. But they *have* been victims of coercion at the hands of government, which keeps them from advancing even further through their own efforts. If we were to think in such terms at all, it would be much more accurate therefore to view benefits as compensation to the poor as innocent victims of the state.

Health Care

The right to health care is perhaps the most widely accepted of all welfare rights.[31] Access to medical care and insurance against the ruinous cost of treating a major illness or injury strike many people as essential elements of freedom because they are literally matters of life and death. Without some measure of health, it is argued, one cannot exploit or enjoy any other opportunity. The loss of health can make it impossible for one to work, carry out family responsibilities, travel, or pursue many other goals in life.

In the end, however, that argument is flawed in the same way as any other appeal to the notion of positive liberty. Obtaining treatment for illness or injury is obviously a human need, but hardly a more important need than obtaining food or shelter. As with all other goals, people need the freedom to weigh it against other goals and to choose the means of obtaining it. But they cannot define their freedom in defiance of the facts, or at the expense of the freedom of others. Illness and injury are natural risks inherent in life, and all the means of dealing with them—from aspirin, to open-heart surgery, to health maintenance organizations—must be produced by human effort to which no one can have a right without the producers' consent.

The belief in a right to health care is also fueled by the increasing cost of medical goods such as hospital stays, doctors' visits, and insurance policies, and by the difficulties that specific groups of people have in obtaining care or insurance. Those problems have been offered as evidence that the market for health care has failed, that health care is not like other economic goods that can be produced and exchanged by voluntary trade, and that government intervention in one form or another is required to solve the problems. Nothing could be further from the truth. Health care is one of the most heavily regulated industries, with layer upon layer of regulations and subsidies, built up over decades, all of them enacted in the name of a right to health care, and all of them contributing to a network of coercive restraints on individuals. The widely publicized problems of cost and access are themselves the result of previous government actions that have interfered with people's freedom to act. The industry is a particularly clear example of the fact that implementing welfare rights means the sacrifice of real liberty.

Government intervention has distorted the market for health care so thoroughly for the past half century that an effort is required to imagine what a genuinely free system would be like. In a system based solely on the classical rights of liberty, property, and contract, patients would be free to choose the type of care they wanted, and the particular health care providers they wanted to see, in accordance with their needs and resources. Doctors and other providers would be free to offer their services on whatever terms they chose; fees would be governed not by government fiat but by the freedom of competitors to offer their services for less. Individuals and families would be free to choose whether they wanted health insurance and, if so, in what amounts. Insurers would provide policies covering different types of medical conditions and services, in accordance with the willingness of consumers to pay for such coverage. Most people would probably buy health insurance directly from insurance companies—the way they buy life, auto, or homeowners insurance—so they would not have to fear that losing or changing their job would mean losing their coverage.

When new drugs, products, and procedures were introduced, they would often be expensive at first, as would insurance policies that covered them, and they would thus be used primarily by wealthier people. But the ability of the wealthy to pay for those goods would not worsen the condition of others, and in time the prices would normally fall as they do for other technologies. In effect, the wealthy would pay the lion's share of the upfront research and development costs for goods that would be increasingly available to others. As with any other product, the poor would not be able to afford the same amount or quality of medical care as those with more money, but basic care—and insurance against catastrophic needs—would certainly be available. Before the government came to dominate the industry, doctors were eager to have the working classes as customers, either directly through fee-for-service arrangements or through arrangements with fraternal organizations, employers, and others. For the poorest of the poor, free care has always been available from doctors and hospitals.[32]

Government intervention has distorted this market in three essential ways. The first is the tax policy that makes employer-provided health insurance exempt from income and payroll taxes. This policy was adopted in the 1950s, and, given the increase in effective tax rates since then, it has created a huge incentive to obtain health insurance through one's employer rather than by purchasing an individual policy with after-tax dollars.[33] The second factor is government subsidies for health care, chiefly through Medicaid and Medicare; altogether, governments at all levels spend over $400 billion a year on health care subsidies.[34] The third factor is regulations imposed to deal with problems created by the first two.

One such problem is price inflation. Since 1960 health care costs have increased at nearly twice the rate of general inflation.[35] That is chiefly the result of increased demand on the part of people whose bills are being paid by someone else. For example, in 1964, before Medicaid went into effect, those above the poverty line saw physicians about 20 percent more frequently than did the poor. By 1975 the poor were visiting physicians 18 percent more often than the nonpoor.[36] To recipients of government aid, the services are free. Why not visit the doctor whenever one wants? Why not demand the extra blood test or X-ray?

The same incentive applies to those with insurance provided by their employers. Because of the tax advantage, employees have an incentive to demand the most expensive form of insurance, with low deductibles and copayments, if any; for many people, insurance covers routine care such as annual checkups. Since they are not paying for care out of their own pockets, they have no incentive to economize, to shop around for the lowest prices, or even to inquire about prices. A total of 75 percent of all medical bills is paid by third parties—either insurance companies or government.[37] That is the primary reason for the rapid rise in the consumption of medical services and the accompanying rise in prices. Indeed, the rise in expenditures on different categories of medical goods—such as hospitals, doctors, vision care, and drugs—is directly proportional to the portion of those expenditures paid by third parties.[38]

The rise in prices, along with fraudulent practices on the part of unscrupulous doctors taking advantage of government money, led to an expanding network of coercive controls on medical practice. The chief control, adopted in the 1980s, was a fixed fee that Medicare and Medicaid would pay for treating a specific condition. That fee was set well below the usual price, and doctors and hospitals responded by "cost-shifting": boosting the prices they charged patients with private insurance in order to recoup their losses from patients in government programs. In 1993 Congressional Budget Office director Robert D. Reischauer reported that hospitals were billing patients with private insurance 28 percent more to cover losses from Medicare and Medicaid patients.[39]

To avoid being victimized in that way, employers, who pay for the bulk of private health insurance, have increasingly replaced fee-for-service arrangements (in which patients and doctors determine amounts and prices of services per visit) with managed care (under which providers typically get a fixed fee for each person enrolled and doctors must get authorization from the insurer before providing treatment). At the same time, many physicians have stopped taking Medicare and Medicaid patients because the fees do not cover their costs. State and federal law severely limits, where it does not abolish, the freedom of the elderly enrolled in Medicare to pay doctors out of their own pocket. As a result, many elderly people are being deprived of services for which they are able and willing to pay.

The system of employer-provided insurance, an artifact of tax policy, has also imposed costs on people who lose their jobs or change jobs and must therefore obtain a new insurance policy. A medical problem that arose under the previous policy becomes a "pre-existing condition" that may raise the price of a new policy or make the person uninsurable—a problem that would not arise if people bought health insurance individually and carried it with them from job to job.

To deal with that problem, governments are adding another layer of regulation: "guaranteed issue" laws, which require insurers to accept anyone, regardless of condition. A number of states have passed such bills, and the federal Kennedy-Kassebaum law of 1996 mandated the guaranteed issue of group health policies to small businesses. A recent report from the General Accounting Office says that the bill is driving up premiums by as much as 125 percent.[40] Another common regulation called "community rating" requires insurance companies to offer policies for the same price to all people, regardless of age, lifestyle, or physical condition. Since the actual risks depend on those very factors, what community rating means is that the young are forced to subsidize the elderly, the well to subsidize the sick, and those with healthy lifestyles to subsidize those with unhealthy ones.

To grasp the kind of coercive transfer involved, consider the effects of guaranteed issue and community rating in New York State, where they were enacted in 1993. Before the new law, a 55-year-old male could obtain an individual health care policy from Mutual of Omaha for $180 per month; the same policy would cost his 25-year-old son just $82. After the law took effect, both paid the same price, $136, a savings for the father but a steep increase for the son. For some younger people, premiums more than doubled. Not surprisingly, some dropped their insurance, either because they could not afford it or because they realized that there was no need to get insurance while they were healthy since the law would guarantee it to them when they got sick. After the first nine months, 25,000 fewer people in New York had insurance, and prices rose because healthy people were leaving the ranks of the insured.[41] In 1994, just a year after the new law, the 55-year-old man was paying $184 per month for his Mutual of Omaha policy, about what he had been paying before the law went into effect, and in 1997 he paid $218. The 25-year-old was forced to pay the same—in the increasingly unlikely event that he wanted to maintain his policy.[42]

Health care, in short, provides an object lesson in how the attempt to secure a welfare right destroys genuine liberty. Government subsidies take hundreds of billions of dollars in taxpayers' money every year—money they are no longer free to spend as they choose. Government actions have driven up medical prices for everyone, and in some cases driven services off the market altogether. The net effect of subsidies, tax policy, and regulations is that doctors are no longer free to offer their services on terms they choose or, in many cases, to prescribe treatment based on their best judgment of the patient's needs; and patients are no longer free to obtain the kinds of care or insurance they choose.

Writing about community rating, Princeton University health economist Uwe Reinhart, an advocate of greater government control of health care, observed, "Community rating violates basic actuarial principles. A community-rated system forces a competing private insurer to look at a deathly ill patient, seeing a $100,000 bill, and cheerfully enroll that person for $2,000. It goes against human nature. So in order to overcome normal human nature, you need some coercion."[43] What Professor Reinhart views as a flaw in human nature, the reluctance to lose $98,000, is in fact a recognition of economic reality. But he is quite correct in his frank admission that this departure from the market is an exercise of coercion, not freedom.

Conclusion

Those who base welfare rights on the concept of positive freedom claim that that concept is an extension of the classical conception of freedom from coercive restraint. The claim is false. The demand for positive freedom is in fact a demand not for freedom but for exemption from a fact of reality: the need to produce in order to consume. Since reality itself offers no such exemption, it can come only from other people. The demand for positive freedom is a demand for coercive transfers from those who produce to those who do not.

That is not to deny that the constraints set by the nature of the world can be as onerous as the constraints imposed coercively by other people. Those who face the former constraints in extreme form—whose unmet needs are pressing and whose means of satisfying them are harsh and few—obviously have a problem to be solved. But it is not the *same* problem as that of people whose poverty and oppression are imposed by a coercive human agency that prevents them from acting to improve their condition. Nor is the solution the same. Protecting genuine freedom is a task that governments can accomplish by enforcing relatively clear and simple rules against the positive use of force and by otherwise staying out of the way. Providing people with well-being and security—expanding their range of alternatives by trying to provide food, shelter, income, education, work, health care, and other goods—is a very different task; and when governments undertake this task they invariably sacrifice genuine freedom. Taxpayers must be forced to pay for the goods, recipients are subjected to coercive terms, and everyone is enmeshed in the web of regulations necessary to make the programs work.

The solution to the problem of unmet needs is production. Individuals must bear the responsibility for acting to produce what they need, and the freedoms they need to do so should be protected:

- the freedom to work for employers willing to hire them, on mutually agreeable terms, without subjection to minimum wage and other coercive restrictions on employment;
- the freedom to start a business without licensing and other coercive restrictions on enterprise;
- the freedom to keep what they have earned, without having to pay through the tax system for social insurance and other public "goods" they do not want; and
- the freedom to purchase housing, medical care, and other goods from willing suppliers without price controls and other coercive restrictions on commerce.

Social scientists have had much more success in answering the question, "What are the causes of wealth?" than the question, "What are the causes of poverty?" The answer to the first question rests on a coherent science: economics. We know that wealth is created through production, trade, the division of labor, the investment of capital, and the invention of new technologies and procedures. But social scientists have met with no such success in explaining poverty. For all the books, studies, and articles in learned journals, for all the data that have been collected and all the hypotheses put forward, the explanation of poverty remains speculative and rife with controversy.

The reason for that disparity lies partly in the fact that human beings have only recently, in certain parts of the world, taken definite actions to create wealth. Against the backdrop of millennia of human history, it is wealth that stands out and calls for explanation. Poverty is simply the absence of wealth. It is the natural human condition, which persists in the absence of efforts to overcome it. Why do some individuals put forth the effort when others do not? Why do some succeed when others do not? Here lies the other reason for the disparity. Those last questions do not admit of general answers. Individuals act or fail to act from countless motives. They are subject to myriad social influences, arising from causes far removed in time and place as well as from the actions of their neighbors. They are also capable of initiating action, exploiting opportunities, and creating new ones within at least a delimited sphere. Scholars can trace the effects of particular factors on specific groups of people, drawing on a dizzying abundance of data. But we cannot tally the effects of all the influences on a given person, much less on all the people in a society. The reality is far too complex for that. This is why there is no science of poverty.

It is best to restrict the concept of freedom to the exercise of choice among the opportunities at hand, and to restrict the concept of coercion to the deliberate interference with that choice by other people. One thing we do know, after all, is that the freedom to acquire and use property, to earn an income, to trade freely with others, is at least a necessary condition for escaping poverty. It muddies the water to say that a person is coerced by the operation of impersonal economic forces, or by his own lack of ability or ambition.

5. Welfare and Benevolence

The transfer of wealth involved in entitlement programs, as we saw in the previous chapter, cannot be justified by appeal to the American political tradition of individual liberty. To many people, however, the appeal to positive freedom is not the core issue. The core issue, rather, is benevolence. A decent person feels compassion for another and tries to help; a decent society should do likewise. The welfare state is simply a collective way to help those in need, a public expression of individual generosity and a way of extending that generosity beyond the range of personal connections. Those who reject the concept of a right to public aid and who propose to cut spending on poverty programs are routinely denounced as selfish, mean, and stingy. "American voters," editorialized the *New York Times*, "want more efficient social spending and a return to bedrock values of family and community. But one of those values is compassion."[1]

This strand in the moral case for the welfare state bypasses the concepts of freedom and coercion that are central to the political tradition of the last 200 years and appeals directly to an older ethical tradition of sharing and benevolence.[2] It is an altruistic ethic that regards the need of one person as a moral claim on others and regards selflessness, compassion, and generosity as primary moral virtues. As we saw in Chapter 3, the revival of the altruist ethic in the last century, as a reaction against Enlightenment individualism and the pursuit of self-interest, was a primary cause of the birth of the welfare state. The same ethic is undoubtedly still the chief reason for popular support of welfare programs.

To evaluate this element in the case for welfare, we need to understand the relationships among benevolence, altruism, and the claims that the needs of others make upon us. We will see that benevolence, properly understood, does not provide any rationale for government programs to transfer wealth. We will go on to examine the ways in which private philanthropy is a more effective expression of genuine benevolence than are the coercive programs of the welfare state.

Benevolence

Altruism, Self-Interest, and Production

> Blessed are the poor in spirit: for theirs is the kingdom of heaven. . . .
> Blessed are the meek: for they shall inherit the earth. . . .
> And if any man will sue thee at the law, and take away thy coat, let him have thy cloak also. . . .
> Give to him that asketh thee, and from him that would borrow of thee turn not thou away. . . .
> If thou wilt be perfect, go and sell that thou hast, and give to the poor, and thou shalt have treasure in heaven. . . .

Those statements from the Gospel of Matthew suggest that the essence of virtue is to deny ourselves, to sacrifice our interests, and to accept suffering on behalf of our fellows. The pursuit of self-interest, by that standard, is at best morally neutral and is often wicked.

Whether it is expressed in religious or in secular forms, the principle of altruism is an important element in popular morality. It is reflected in the attitude that service and sacrifice are the essence of nobility. A popular newspaper columnist writes, "I'm put off when adults ask children the inane question: what do you want to be when you grow up? Ask instead, how do you want to serve society?"[3] A critic of religious conservatives asks rhetorically, "Is today's religious right injecting a Christian spirit of compassion and selflessness into American politics?" Citing the religious right's support for welfare cuts, he answers no.[4]

Conservatives themselves are sensitive to the charge. Peter Wehner, director of policy at Empower America, observes that a central message of the New Testament is the danger of wealth. "Christ knew the insidiously strong pull that riches exert on our heart and affections. . . . The demands Christ places on our lives are far more radical than most of us—certainly than I—want to admit."[5] Moral ambivalence about wealth is indeed another consequence of the altruist ethic. The profit motive is sometimes respected but almost never praised. Though America has a commercial culture that generally esteems business success, a vein of hostility toward wealth lies just below the surface. It breaks through in the form of popular resentment in times of economic turmoil, and in response to those whose motives are too nakedly self-interested.

For people who espouse altruism, motives are indeed the object of intense, even obsessive concern. Actions that in fact benefit others lose their moral luster if the gain to others was not the primary object. "Insofar as one is acting primarily in the interest of increasing profit," writes a philosopher, "it is trivially true that one's primary interest is not in doing what is morally right."[6] Nor is monetary reward the only form of morally discrediting benefit. At Chapel Hill High School in North Carolina, where students must do community service work in order to graduate, a student was denied credit for building benches for a local nature trail because he got Boy Scout credit toward his merit badges, a benefit deemed incompatible with the principle of service.[7] Even the desire for knowledge can be viewed as selfish. Bryan Molloy, a developer of the anti-depressant drug Prozac, was asked in an interview how he felt about discovering something that has helped so many people. "I just wanted to do it for the intellectual high," he said. "It looked like scientific fun." The interviewer was disappointed that Molloy's efforts in the laboratory had not been a sacrifice: "Reality is rarely what we imagine. Great and noble things do not always happen for great and noble reasons."[8]

There is an obvious question, however, to ask about the ethic of altruism: Why *should* self-denial be a virtue? If it is wrong to act for one's own interests, why is it right to act for the interests of others? Why is it noble to value the lives and happiness of others, but not one's own? If knowledge, wealth, joy, and the relief of suffering are good for human beings, why is it better to provide those benefits to others than to achieve them for oneself?[9]

Those attitudes often spring from the assumption that the interests of people generally conflict, that success is a zero-sum game in which one person's gain is another's loss, that the stronger and more able flourish at the expense of the weaker and less able. If interests do conflict, then life presents us with a choice between sacrificing the interests of others to the pursuit of our own or sacrificing our interests on behalf of others. Society must make benevolence, generosity, service, and self-sacrifice the central virtues it enshrines in the moral lessons it teaches and in the examples it holds up for admiration, lest the grounds for cooperation and peaceful coexistence be destroyed by conflict, lest man become a wolf to man.

The assumption that interests generally conflict rests in turn on another assumption: that individuals must compete for goods existing in more or less fixed quantities. The latter assumption survives from an era when wealth *was* a more or less fixed quantity. The moral codes of most major religions were formed at a time when human beings lived in nomadic bands, or in settlements engaged in primitive agriculture. Through long centuries, economic progress was slow and halting, easily reversed by years of bad harvests or plagues; and wealth was more often acquired by conquest than by production. For over 200 years, however, economists have understood that wealth is not a static quantity. It is continually created through trade and the division of labor, through the investment of productive capital, and through technological innovation. Since the Industrial Revolution, moreover, the gains from innovation and from ever-expanding trade have been spectacular, allowing an ever-growing population to enjoy ever-higher standards of living.

Of course there are still conflicts of interest among individuals and firms over jobs, sales, opportunities, and so on, but such conflicts arise from the operation of an economy that has worked to everyone's benefit. Human beings do not exist in a Darwinian struggle for survival. When individuals or firms compete, what they are competing for is the opportunity to cooperate with buyers or sellers in a mutually beneficial exchange. We no longer live in small clans or communities in which there is only so much to go around, and in which the survival of all depends on the willingness of each to limit the claims of self. The great gains in human welfare have come, not from philanthropists distributing alms among the wretched, but from investors and entrepreneurs seeking opportunities for profit, from inventors seeking new ideas to patent, from specialists seeking to excel in well-paying professions, from workers who apply themselves to earn the best wage they can—in short, from producers of every description seeking their self-interest in a society of trade.

That is not to deny that benevolence, compassion, and generosity are still virtues.[10] There are emergencies that people cannot survive without help. There are handicaps that deserve sympathy and accommodation. But conventional morality has never assimilated the fact that the pursuit of self-interest, and in particular the pursuit of wealth, is not a threat to others or to the social order. Conventional morality has not recognized that the honor due to courage, integrity, and dedication is not diminished when those traits serve a personal end. Most important, it has not recognized that in matters of material well-being, generosity cannot be the primary moral virtue because it depends on the creation of wealth. As Ayn Rand put it,

> Men have been taught that the highest virtue is not to achieve, but to give. Yet one cannot give that which has not been created. Creation comes before distribution—or there will be nothing to distribute. The need of the creator comes before the need of any possible beneficiary. Yet we are taught to admire the second-hander who dispenses gifts he has not produced above the man who made the gifts possible. We praise an act of charity. We shrug at an act of achievement.[11]

The measure of a good society, accordingly, is not merely—nor primarily—the benefits extended to the poor, even to the deserving poor who are unable to provide for their own needs, as some moralists have argued.[12] The primary measure of a good society is the scope it affords achievement—the freedom society allows the able, the ambitious, and the productive to create value—value of any kind, from the production of material wealth, to the discovery of scientific knowledge, to the creation of art. It is from such achievements that all benefits flow, both to the creators and to others. Benevolence is a virtue, but it is not the primary virtue. It must yield pride of place to courage, integrity, rationality, dedication, and the other virtues that make achievement possible.

Benevolence versus Altruism

Even if generosity and charity are not primary, it may be argued, they are still good things for an individual or a society. Granted that the able should be free to achieve and to reap the rewards of their achievements, don't the less able have a right to share in those rewards? Isn't there some obligation to help those in need, an obligation discharged through the welfare state? After all, as philosopher Jeremy Waldron argues,

> Charity is usually understood as a person giving part of his wealth to others who are less well-off than he is. The welfare state can be seen as an institutionalization of such giving, with the important qualifications that the donation is compulsory, collected as taxation, and that the nature and destination of the tax or "gift" is not under the direct control of

95

the giver. The welfare state, to put it crudely, is a form of government-directed charity.[13]

But those "qualifications" make all the difference. There are two radically different ways of providing relief for poverty and economic misfortune: private philanthropy and government programs. The first system is voluntary, the second coercive. The first operates through the institutions of civil society: families, churches, mutual-aid societies, and private charities. The second operates through the transfer programs of the state. The first is an expression of the donor's benevolence, the second an expression of the recipient's right.

The last is the essential point. The exercise of compassion through private, voluntary charity leaves the donor free to choose whether he wishes to contribute, and to whom, and subject to what conditions. It leaves him as owner of his resources and makes any help he gives others a free gift. It is precisely this freedom that the concept of a right to welfare is intended to eliminate. A right is an entitlement. If someone has a right to medical care, for example, then he is entitled to the time, the effort, the ability, the wealth of whoever is going to be forced to provide that care. In effect, he *owns* a piece of the taxpayers who subsidize him and the doctors who tend to him. A doctor who waives his bill for an indigent patient is offering a free gift; he retains his autonomy, and the patient owes him gratitude. But if the patient has a right to care, then the doctor is merely giving him his due.

As we saw in Chapter 2, the classical rights of life, liberty, and property are rights to action, not to goods per se. So one person's rights impose on other people only the negative obligation not to interfere with him, not to restrain him forcibly from acting as he chooses. One person's right to life, for example, means that no one may take his life, or assault or enslave him, but others do not have the positive obligation to help him live. The negative character of these obligations was part of the classical conception of rights. But welfare rights impose *positive* obligations on others. A welfare right by nature is a right to a positive outcome, not contingent on the success of one's own efforts. It must therefore impose on others the obligation to ensure that outcome. A right to health care, education, housing, a minimum income, or other such goods imposes on someone the obligation to provide those goods, normally through the tax system that funds the welfare state.

To appreciate the stark moral difference between charity and rights, consider the biblical story of the Good Samaritan who comes to the aid of a stranger lying beaten and robbed on the highway. Here is the very paradigm of charity: a victim suffers through no fault of his own, his need is temporary but intense, the Samaritan can help at little cost or risk to himself. Extending help in such a case is surely admirable, and we may feel contempt for the other passers-by in the story who will not lift a finger to help. Anglo-American law, however, has traditionally refused to compel Good Samaritan behavior. It has not conferred on the victim a right to aid. In this respect at least, the law regards every individual as an end in himself, a self-owner, with the moral right to live for himself and to choose whether, when, and how he will offer his services to others. To compel such service, even in a case of extreme need, is to impose a form of involuntary servitude.

In moral terms, welfare programs amount to compulsory Good Samaritanism. Suppose it were argued that, out of compassion for those in need, every citizen should be compelled to work seven hours per week as a "volunteer" in a hospital, poverty center, or institution for the disabled. (Seven hours is 17.5 percent of a 40-hour work week and represents about the same proportion of taxable income that goes to support the welfare state.) In the sphere of private philanthropy, after all, people do contribute their time as well as their money. If government programs are simply a collective way to organize charitable activities, why not compel both sorts of contributions? Why not support welfare programs through a kind of "draft" as well as through taxes? Such proposals have in fact been made from time to time, usually in the form of national service requirements for the young. Such proposals illustrate the same principle as compulsory Good Samaritanism: by compelling a form of involuntary servitude, they negate the individual's right to his own life.

The same is true of the forcible transfer of money in the form of taxes. To be sure, a legal duty to pay 17.5 percent of my income leaves me free to decide how to spend my time; a tax is a less intrusive violation of my freedom than is a draft. But the same principle is at stake. I need to earn a living; that is not an arbitrary choice on my part. As philosopher Robert Nozick has argued, taxes that take 17.5 percent of a person's income mean that he is compelled to spend 17.5 percent of his productive time working for others involuntarily.[14] The difference between such compulsory "donation" and forced labor is one of degree, not kind.

The more honest defenders of the welfare state accept this implication. Philosopher Richard Arneson claims that "in some circumstances, forced labor can be a morally acceptable state policy" because the needy have a genuine ownership right in the productive members of society—an ownership right that, he acknowledges, is comparable to the right that feudal lords claimed in their serfs. Whether the right is exercised through taxes or forced labor is a secondary concern.[15] In a similar vein, philosopher Rodney Peffer conducts the following thought experiment: An "ailing but greatly loved violinist" has kidney failure, and you are the only person with the right blood type to save him, but only if you remain physically attached through tubes that allow his blood to circulate through your kidneys. "I . . . wish to assert that the violinist has a (prima facie) right to life and hence to the necessities of life and, in these particular circumstances, a (prima facie) right to the use of your kidneys." That "prima facie" right, Peffer acknowledges, is overridden by the fact that such a great sacrifice would be required on your part, but if the sacrifice were smaller the violinist's right would take precedence and you could be forced to aid him.[16] Neither Arneson nor Peffer offers reasons for his views. They appeal instead to their readers' feelings about what is right, feelings shaped by a culture in which altruism has played a major part.

Thus the idea of a right to welfare goes far beyond charity. It makes aid to others a duty. It makes the need of recipients an enforceable claim on the wealth of potential donors. And, when we think it through, it implies that recipients have an ownership right in the ability and effort of those who produce wealth. The rationale for this claim must therefore go far beyond the principle that generosity is a virtue. In fact, behind all the references to compassion, generosity, and empathy, the real basis of welfare rights is a form of the principle of altruism that denies the very basis of individual rights.

"The basic principle of altruism," notes Ayn Rand, "is that man has no right to exist for his own sake, that service to others is the only justification of his existence, and that self-sacrifice is his highest moral duty, virtue, and value."[17] Altruism holds that the individual does not have a moral right to live for himself; he has a duty to serve others. It holds that others have a moral claim on his productive ability, the fruits of which he may enjoy only on condition that his efforts benefit others as well. It holds that his ability, initiative, intelligence, dedication to his goals, and all the other qualities that make success possible are personal liabilities as well as assets, putting him under an obligation to those with less ability, initiative, intelligence, or dedication. This principle is the basis for holding that individuals have positive obligations to support one another, and thus that one person's need constitutes a right to the resources of another.

But why should someone have an unchosen duty to serve others— not because he values them as friends, not because he has incurred obligations to them by his own actions, but simply because they exist? Why should another's need—the absence of the ability to support himself—constitute a positive claim on the wealth and ability of those who can produce? Granted that the strong should not prey on the weak, where do the weak get the right to be carried by the strong? Ability, wealth, and success often make people generous, as an expression of pride in themselves and benevolence toward the world in which they have flourished. But how can one justify the idea that such people literally owe a portion of their ability to the unable, a portion of their wealth to the poor, a portion of their success to those who have not succeeded? By what logic can a lack be transmuted into an entitlement?

The moral code of altruism, and the notion of a right to welfare that is based upon it, is incompatible with the principle that the individual is an end in himself who may not be used against his will. This principle is the core of Enlightenment individualism and one of its historical achievements. Throughout most of man's history, society was governed by more or less despotic rulers, who regarded their subjects as resources. It was commonly assumed that the individual belonged to society: to the tribe, the city, the nation, the feudal lord, or the king. Rulers have always insisted that their purposes were more important than those of their subjects, and they have acted accordingly on the presumption that the time, effort, money, and even the lives of their subjects could be sacrificed in the pursuit of conquest, prestige, or other royal ends. The concept of individual rights deflated this attitude with the question, "Important to whom?" It recognized that every individual person is a locus of value; for each of us, our own lives and happiness are ends in themselves. As John Locke put it, we each have a property in our persons: our lives, our labor, our time and talent belong to us as individuals. This is the core meaning of the right to life.

The concept of welfare rights represents a new twist on the old conception of the individual as a resource to be used for the ends of others. It is not the ends of the rulers—the strong and powerful— but the ends of the weak and powerless for which ordinary people are to be used. It is no longer the feudal masters but the poor, the elderly, and the disabled who claim ownership rights in those who produce. The concept of welfare rights does not represent a historic advance in moral development, as its advocates often assert. It represents a reversion to a primitive moral code.

Charity as a Value Rather Than a Duty

Once we reject the concept of a right to welfare, we can understand aid to the poor, not as an obligation for donors to discharge, but as a value for them to pursue as their means allow. It was during the 19th century, against the background of increasing wealth for an increasing proportion of the population, that poverty began to seem unnatural, a problem to be solved. And that concern produced a vast profusion and variety of philanthropic efforts. The same factors that promoted concern for poverty a century ago exist today on a much larger scale—our society is that much wealthier. Charity is one of the values on which people can and will choose to spend the money they have earned. Thus the question is not, How can we be sure to extract from people everything they owe to others? The question is, Under what conditions can people most effectively pursue the value of helping others? As with the pursuit of any other value, however, we start with a clear recognition that donors should be free to make their own decisions about the use of their money.

They should be free to choose the portion of their income they wish to devote to this value in relation to their other values, or the portion of their time they wish to contribute as volunteers. They should be free to choose the particular objects of their benevolence: some people want to contribute specifically to the homeless, others to unwed mothers, others to the elderly poor, others to promising students who could not otherwise afford college. They should be free to choose whether to contribute primarily within their own community or to national or international causes. They should be free to make judgments about what they think are the most effective instruments for providing aid—religious or secular charities, scholarships provided by schools or by foundations, fraternal-society aid, and so on.

And, most important, they must choose who deserves their aid. It is one thing to help a recently widowed or divorced mother who is struggling to get past a temporary crisis in her life; it is another thing to help a woman who uses her children as a ticket to a work-free way of life on welfare. It is one thing to help someone disabled by an accident, another to help someone "disabled" by taking drugs.

Government now makes most of those decisions for us. The welfare state has, in effect, nationalized the charity industry. The government decides how much income shall be taken for transfers, and how the resulting pool of tax revenues will be distributed among the various categories of recipients. A single decision on these matters is made on behalf of all donor-taxpayers, each of whom has a minute chance of affecting the decision through his individual vote.

For the reasons we have explored, the system of government-run charity is immoral: the obligations it imposes on those who pay the bills are not consistent with the recognition of individuals as ends in themselves. Those same reasons also make government-run charity ineffective. The coercive character of government welfare programs makes it virtually impossible for them to provide the kind of help that the poor need, and the voluntary character of private philanthropy makes it a more effective alternative. The second half of this chapter will confirm and illustrate those propositions.

Public versus Private Aid

The Need to Distinguish the Problems of Public Aid

Charity is the effort to help those in need. But need varies. Sometimes it is brief but intense, the product of an emergency like a hurricane or fire, and the victims need only temporary support to restore their normal, self-supporting lives. Other people are in need as a result of longer term mental or physical disabilities, and a longer term investment is necessary if they are to realize whatever potential they can. Need can arise from sheer bad luck, from factors truly outside the person's control; emergencies are once again the obvious example. At the other extreme, the straitened circumstances in which some people live are entirely their own doing, the result of abandoning responsibility for their lives. Most cases fall in between the extremes; poverty is the result of bad luck and bad choices in various degrees. As Alexis de Tocqueville observed, "Nothing is so difficult to distinguish as the nuances which separate unmerited misfortune from an adversity produced by vice. How many miseries are simultaneously the result of both these causes!"[18]

For that reason, effective charity requires discrimination among cases and the use of measures adapted to the circumstances of the people one is trying to help. This was a central theme of 19th-century philanthropy. Relief workers in that era, especially in America, generally opposed government charity, like the British Poor Law, because it encouraged idleness, teaching the populace that income was possible without work. "Gratuitous aid," wrote New York charity worker John Griscom, produces a "relaxation of concern on the part of the poor to depend on their own foresight and industry."[19] Many of the settlement houses and missions had "work tests"—men were expected to chop wood, women to sew, before they received meals or lodging—as a way of distinguishing freeloaders from people willing to take responsibility for themselves.[20]

Governments find it extremely difficult to draw such distinctions. They simply provide benefits amounting to an alternative way of life for those at the bottom of the economic ladder, with no regard for merit and little regard for circumstance. Though welfare benefits hardly provide a comfortable existence, and benefit levels in some programs such as Aid to Families with Dependent Children had declined in real terms, the package of benefits in many states was more attractive than entry-level work. On the eve of the 1996 welfare reform bill, Michael Tanner of the Cato Institute and his associates studied the total package of benefits available as entitlements. They found that AFDC, food stamps, and Medicaid benefits went to virtually all participants in federally supported welfare. Smaller numbers enjoyed public housing (23 percent), utility assistance (50 percent), and nutrition programs (56 percent). The study compared benefit levels with the annual income and hourly wage necessary to provide the same after-tax income, both for the full package of benefits and for just the three basic ones. The results vary from state to state, but Table 5.1 shows the ranges.

TABLE 5.1

WAGE EQUIVALENTS OF WELFARE BENEFITS (DOLLARS)

| | Full Package | | | AFDC, Food Stamps, Medicaid | | |
	Total Benefits	Yearly Income Equiv.	Hourly Wage Equiv.	Total Benefits	Yearly Income Equiv.	Hourly Wage Equiv.
High	27,736	36,100	17	19,071	21,300	10
Median	17,780	19,100	9	11,797	10,100	5
Low	13,033	11,500	6	7,353	6,100	3

Sources: Michael Tanner, Stephen Moore, and David Hartman, "The Work vs. Welfare Trade-Off," Cato Institute Policy Analysis no. 240, September 19, 1995, pp. 18 (Table 8), 21 (Table 9), 30 (Table 15). Some figures are from revisions reported in Michael Tanner and Naomi Lopez, "The Value of Welfare," Cato Institute Briefing Paper no. 27, June 12, 1996. These benefits were calculated for a single mother with two children and did not include any disability benefits under Supplemental Security Income.

It is evident that, despite the variation, even the basic package exceeds minimum wage work in the upper range of states and the full package exceeds that level in all states.

In a major study of welfare participation, Robert Moffitt found that material incentives make a difference. One measure of the difference is the proportion of people eligible for means-tested programs who actually apply for and receive them. Since the 1960s, the "participation rate" has roughly tracked the level of benefits; the evidence "strongly suggests that [the caseload explosion of the 1960s–1970s] was the result of benefit growth of AFDC in the early 1960s and of the benefit sum thereafter." Another way to measure the effect of welfare on material incentives is to look at the amount of work that welfare recipients do to boost their incomes. Although few people actually leave jobs to go on welfare, those already receiving benefits earn about 37 cents less for every additional dollar they receive in transfers.[21]

None of this is to say that a life on welfare is attractive. The welfare system is demeaning. It imposes on recipients every roadblock and indignity the bureaucratic mind can conceive.[22] The problem is that both the benefits and the drawbacks fall upon the worthy and the unworthy alike. Government programs are unable to draw the distinctions necessary for effective charity because of four factors inherent in their nature *as* government programs:

1. If welfare is provided by the government in a modern liberal society, it must be construed as a right; it cannot depend on the personal virtues or vices of recipients or their willingness to take responsibility for themselves.
2. Since the state is the agency of coercion, its actions must be governed by the rule of law. Government bureaucrats cannot be given discretionary power to discriminate among recipients on the basis of personal morality or psychology.
3. As the agency of coercion, the government of a free country must also refrain from intruding into the personal dimensions of life, and this precludes the kind of active involvement often required for effective help.
4. Because government programs are bureaucratic and subject to the political process, they cannot have the flexibility to adapt to change, the spirit of innovation, and the diversity of approaches that private agencies have.

Each of those factors calls for a closer look.

Rights versus Responsibility. It is inherent in the nature of a government benefit that recipients have at least a statutory right to it, and this has been the explicit goal of most welfare advocates. In the 1940s Donald Howard of the Russell Sage Foundation sought to create a structure of rights to welfare so that "no person would have the discretionary power to deny to any eligible applicant the aid to which he is entitled."[23] The attorney for the welfare clients in the *Smith v. King* case (1968) explicitly sought, and received from Chief Justice Earl Warren, a ruling "interpreting the Social Security Act as having rejected the concept of a worthy and an unworthy poor."[24]

If one creates legal entitlements, however, one is promoting an entitlement mentality. There is no escape from this logic. If anyone who meets conditions of eligibility is entitled to support, if the causes of a person's condition are irrelevant, then the message to the poor is: We will stand between you and reality and cushion you from the consequences of your actions. It doesn't matter why you had the baby, you have it now and we'll send a check. It doesn't matter whether you lost your job because of a layoff or because you never showed up on time; you're out of work and we'll send you a check. As a Philadelphia clergyman observed in the last century, "[T]he state, as the institute of rights, can give nothing to any man without conceding that it is his right to have it. Therefore, the state is the worst dispenser of alms. . . . Every dollar it spends on the relief of the poor, is an admission that they have the right to be supported at the public expense, whether their need be due to idleness and improvidence, or to a blameless failure to succeed in life."[25]

That admission encourages the entitlement mentality, and anecdotes from the daily news suggest how pervasive it is:

- A Kentucky welfare case worker reports, "Here's a couple who just reapplied. He's 30, unemployed. She's 25 and works at a local day care center. When they brought in their checking account, it showed $36 a month for each of them to belong to a fitness center. Some people just don't know how to budget. . . . They're not making ends meet, and they want to keep their HBO and call-waiting."[26]
- Sandra White, a workfare garbage collector in New York City, said her "job was in no way giving her dignity or valuable work experience, especially since she worked seven years for a commercial bank until she was laid off. She also accused the Giuliani administration of dissembling when it insists that workfare participants are receiving training for permanent private sector jobs. 'There's no training whatever,' she said. 'You have to work in the rain and not complain. This is slavery.' "[27]
- "Maurice B. Tiff, a 47-year-old portrait artist from Cleveland, has lived with his elderly parents while receiving general assistance benefits intermittently since 1991. He acknowledges that he can survive without the monthly $100 check and that he has continued to reapply successfully for benefits because no one has stopped him from doing so. In essence, Mr. Tiff said, he works when he feels like it, while taking care of his parents. 'It's not that I'm not capable or willing,' he said. 'I'm probably one person who shouldn't have been on general assistance to begin with.' "[28]
- "When four Dutch sociologists interviewed hundreds of people in three Dutch cities, they found that about 55 percent of the long-term unemployed in their sample had stopped looking for

work. More than half this group had quit because they had found 'other activities to give meaning to their lives: hobbies voluntary work, studying, or working in the informal economy.' "[29]

- Karen Schaumann, a welfare rights activist in Michigan, asserts, "We have a right to survive, our kids have a right to survive, poor women have a right to have babies."[30]

In one way or another, each of those cases illustrates a failure to take responsibility for one's life. Responsible people know that results cannot be obtained without effort. One cannot expect income without work, or work without education and training. Responsible people also know they must deal with the consequences of their actions and circumstances, reducing their spending on luxuries when their income drops, when they have a child, and the like. The relationships between cause and effect are not imposed by anyone's arbitrary edict. They are "imposed" by reality. Responsible people are willing to accept and deal with reality directly without asking others to intervene for them, in the way parents intervene for their children. The delicate task of philanthropy is to provide temporary support and training without reinforcing the tendencies to irresponsibility exhibited by the previous examples. It is essential, above all, that such help be conditional, not given as an entitlement. But government programs by their very nature can give benefits only as an entitlement.

Many people on welfare do not succumb to the inducements to irresponsibility, and it is a credit to their character that they do not. A majority of welfare recipients stay on welfare for relatively brief spells, after a divorce or between jobs. Because the short-term users come and go, however, the majority of those on welfare at any one time are long-term dependents. If the welfare system were a hotel, most of the people checking in during a given week would be staying for a few days, but as they came and went they would be using a small number of rooms. Most of the rooms would be occupied by long-term residents who had checked in much earlier.

Mary Jo Bane and David Elwood found that of the people *entering* the welfare rolls at a given point in time, 55 percent will spend less than four years on welfare during their lives, while under a third, 29 percent, will spend eight years or more. Of those *receiving* welfare at a given point in time, however, only 19 percent will spend four years or less, while two-thirds, 66 percent, will spend eight years or more.[31] In other words, the bulk of welfare expenditures goes to people who are chronic dependents. A huge welfare industry has been trying to devise ways of making them self-supporting, by offering incentives, counseling, work-training programs, day care, and so on. But as long as the basic benefits are offered as entitlements, the result is only to infantilize the poor: as is done for children, their environment is being structured to mimic responsibility without exposure to real consequences.

Private agencies, by contrast, increasingly recognize the need to replace automatic help with contracts specifying terms that recipients must meet in order to receive help. This is especially true of shelters for the homeless, which deal with the toughest cases: many of the homeless are substance abusers who have been exploiting both public and private agencies—selling food stamps, getting free meals to conserve cash, and so forth—in order to obtain money for drugs and alcohol. At the Center for the Homeless in South Bend, Indiana, those seeking help must agree to abide by a strict set of rules; to receive any aid beyond the minimum, they must work with a case worker to create a plan for becoming self-sufficient. At Step 13 in Denver, those seeking shelter must agree to take Antabuse (a drug that causes sickness if one consumes alcohol) and submit to drug tests; and they can be expelled for disruptive behavior. Above and beyond the specific rationales for those rules, they convey the message that help is conditional, not an entitlement, and that irresponsibility will have consequences.

Rule of Law. To make aid conditional, and thus to help those on welfare become truly self-sufficient, programs must take account of the differences among recipients, tailoring benefits so that only those with the motivation to become independent receive straight grants, and those without that motivation are given help—if at all—only with strings attached. But this poses a problem that is inherent in the nature of government programs. "Inspired by norms of equal treatment and welfare entitlement," one scholar writes, "a democratic government often finds it awkward to accept the need for tailored policies and target-specific programs."[32] Such policies and programs are much more than "awkward," however. They conflict with the rule of law.

A basic principle of our legal system is that since the state is the agency of coercion, its actions must be bound by universal, objective law. If we are to be ruled by laws and not by men, government officials cannot be given discretionary power in applying the law, treating cases differently as they see fit. Laws must be applied fairly, and that means they must be applied as mechanically as possible. We generally associate the conception of the rule of law with the state's power to define and punish crimes. But it also applies to the more ambitious and less easily defined tasks that governments have taken on—including welfare programs.

As citizens of the nation, potential recipients of government benefits have a civil right to have those benefits distributed by some definite rule, not by the whim of program administrators. To the extent that welfare programs comply with the rule of law, therefore, they cannot discriminate among recipients on the basis of personal morality or psychology, which are not subject to formulation in terms the law can work with. Yet those are precisely the factors that must be addressed to get people to become self-supporting and to deny benefits to the chronically irresponsible.

The failure of government programs to make that distinction is demoralizing to those who are trying to become self-supporting:

- "On this bright, chilly morning, Ms. Diaz has been up all night with [her daughter], who is running a fever. She thinks the government should evaluate each welfare case on an individual basis. People like her, who are going to work or school, have only two or three kids, and are trying to become self-sufficient, should be entitled to the extra help, she says. But, she adds, 'these people having six, seven, eight, nine kids at home and sitting on their tail—they shouldn't get nothing.' "[33]
- "Toni Brown, a 24-year-old single mother receiving $169 in food stamps each month, is living in a subsidized two-bedroom apartment in Shelbyville with her 4-year-old son Brandon, while she works at Wal-Mart and attends the University of Louisville, 38 miles away. A sophomore majoring in chemistry and Spanish, she has made the Dean's list. . . . Nothing angers her more, she said, than people who milk the system with no intention of quitting. . . . 'It makes me really hot,' she said the other day before picking up Brandon at the Childtown Day Care Center.

'I see them just sit around, watching soapies all day. I see the drug dealers. One girl in my community, a teenager, I heard her say, "When I have my next baby, they'd better give me a three-bedroom apartment." These people have no ambition.' "[34]

The distinction these welfare mothers are drawing is one that should be made, on behalf of recipients of aid as well as donors. It's a distinction that private individuals and agencies *can* make, the kind of moral criterion they can use, *because* they are private. If they make a mistake, recipients can go elsewhere. But public officials must go by objective, public criteria.

The welfare agencies have tried to implement some distinctions. For example, the federal welfare reform bill of 1996 mandated that welfare programs in all states include work "requirements" for certain categories of recipients. But such requirements must be stated in terms of behavioral criteria—enrolling in training class, listing with job agencies, applying for jobs, and the like. Recipients may comply with such rules without any genuine effort to find work (and the requirements always have so many loopholes that they are not really requirements at all). In effect, the requirements become further tests of eligibility for benefits, reconfirming the entitlement mentality. That is why government job-training programs have had such disappointing results. In a comprehensive survey for the Brookings Institution, Gary Burtless found that most programs raised recipients' earnings only modestly and did not move many people off welfare.[35] Douglas Besharov and Karen N. Gardiner studied three demonstration projects for teenage mothers on AFDC—offering job training, education, health care, family planning—and found little improvement in participants as compared with control groups. There was no effect on the likelihood of remaining on welfare and little gain in functional literacy; a majority of the women had repeat pregnancies and bore additional children.[36]

It is clear that getting off welfare and into a job has at least as much to do with character as with skills. As one employer observed,

> For unskilled or semiskilled work, it's not trained people that businesses need; it's dependable, hard workers. Of course, I'd prefer a dependable worker who's already trained if you've got one, but if necessary, just give me an unskilled but dependable person of character, and I'll take care of the rest. . . . I can train a person to disassemble a phone; I can't

train her to not get a bad attitude when she discovers that she's expected to come to work every day when the rest of us are there. I can train a worker to properly handle a PC board; I can't train him to show up for work sober or to respect authority.[37]

Administrators of 19th-century settlement houses who required work effort could make a judgment about the character and motives of the recipients, about the sincerity of their efforts. The same is true of the more successful job-placement efforts of private agencies today. But such discretion cannot safely be given to bureaucrats who wield the power of the state.

Freedom and Welfare. An essential aspect of freedom pertains to the personal sphere of life: the freedom to choose one's domestic and family arrangements and to live and work where one chooses, outside the scope of state observation and control. As the agency of coercion, the state cannot be allowed into this sphere without sacrificing freedom. Yet the kind of active involvement often required for effective help involves just that sort of intervention. As Louis M. Nanni, director of South Bend's Center for the Homeless, observes, "Governments cannot provide the spiritual and assertive solutions that today's social problems increasingly require. But private, community-based groups like ours *can* require drug tests, set living rules, and demand behavioral changes."[38]

Bane and Ellwood note that poverty agencies have at times tried to operate like private social work institutions, becoming involved in the lives of their "clients," counseling, cajoling, and assessing moral character. As an example, they cite instructions for home visits issued in 1963 by the New York State Department of Social Work:

> The worker will obtain much information about the general atmosphere of the home he visits through his ability to observe and to understand what he sees. Are relationships congenial or unfriendly? Does one member of the household hold a dominant or domineering position? Is one over-critical of the others? Are parents or guardians aware of, and interested in meeting, the needs of children?[39]

It is chilling to think of such deeply personal "information" being gathered by agents of the same state that has the coercive power to collect taxes and punish crimes.

The social work model of welfare was replaced during the 1960s by an eligibility or entitlement model, in which agencies became gatekeepers whose chief function was to enforce eligibility rules for benefits. The welfare rights movement of that era insisted that welfare be administered as a right, without discretion or personal judgment by case workers. For example, special grants for furniture or other needs were replaced by consolidated grants that were computed automatically. In 1961 the Department of Health, Education, and Welfare prohibited states from excluding a mother from AFDC if she had an "unsuitable home," the usual criterion being that she was sleeping with a man not the father of her children. HEW had decided, properly, that that was an unsuitable moral judgment for the government to be making.

The pendulum is swinging back now to oversight of the poor and restrictions on them, with governments asserting control over the poor that is frankly paternalistic (and thus makes a mockery of the argument from liberty considered in the last chapter). Massachusetts, to take one of many examples, has created "second-chance homes," residences for young unmarried welfare mothers. The homes provide child care and teach parenting and homemaking skills; they usually require that the young women finish school. "There are rules, rewards and punishments. The mothers must leave their rooms spotless, for daily inspections. They can use pay telephones but are limited to 15 minutes per call. They have to sign in and sign out. There is a 10 p.m. curfew on weekdays and an 11:30 curfew on Fridays and Saturdays. 'As a society,' says Joseph Galiant, Massachusetts state secretary for health and human services, 'we say we've got to take control of these kids who are out there on their own. If there isn't a family there, we're providing the family.'"[40]

There is no denying the need for intervention in the lives of at least some welfare recipients. But it is an intrusive violation of freedom for *government* agencies to be engaged in such intimate realms. The "man-in-the-house" rule, for example, was properly abolished, even though it would not be unreasonable for a private agency to insist on it. Nor would it be unreasonable if a private home for young unmarried mothers adopted, as many have, the rules of the second-chance homes in Massachusetts. Private agencies have no hold over the people they help, who are always free to leave. Of course, welfare recipients can choose not to accept government benefits with strings attached, just as they can turn down benefits from private agencies. But to the extent that government has nationalized the charity industry, it has deprived the poor of this option by appropriating funds that would otherwise be available for private philanthropy.

Taxpayers, moreover, do not have the option of withholding support from programs they consider ineffective or wrong. It has become increasingly clear that any program to help the most vulnerable and dependent welfare recipients must deal with values and personal convictions. Some states are already using the new powers granted them by the 1996 welfare reform law to experiment with church-based programs that combine material support, job training, and religious instruction. Michigan, for example, funds programs with the Salvation Army and Good Samaritan Ministries to match welfare recipients with church members who serve as mentors. The executive director of Good Samaritan acknowledges that his goal is religious conversion. "As a Christian, that's my desire for society as a whole. I have a professional opportunity to bear that out with the cooperation of the government."[41] Taxpayers are being forced to contribute to the advocacy of religious faith and to recruitment of members by religious sects.

If those programs were entirely private, no one could object. But state funding, and the supervision that necessarily accompanies it, breaches the separation of church and state. It violates the freedom of taxpayers to choose what doctrines they will support and threatens to undermine the autonomy of religious institutions.

Monopoly versus Diversity. An important factor in the rise of the welfare state, as we saw in Chapter 3, was confidence in the rationality of state action. Complaining of the messy, "patchwork" character of private philanthropy, reformers sought first to have private programs replaced by government ones, and then to have state-level activities replaced by a single federal system. Their arguments were the same as those of the socialists who wanted to nationalize economic industries: they complained on the one hand of "wasteful duplication" inherent in competition and, on the other, of the lack of conscious, deliberate oversight of the allocation of resources. The socialists thought that a national government could rationally plan how to allocate capital and other resources within a single, monopolistic system of production. In the same way, the welfare statists thought—and many still think—that the welfare agencies of the national government could rationally determine how to aid the poor within a single, monopolistic system of distribution. But that view should join socialism in the dustbin of history.

The director of the Washington office of the Council of Jewish Federations complains that voluntary donors are unreliable: "People tend to give to their favorite charities, but their favorite charities may not be the ones that need it most. Services for children may get lots of money; disabled people's services may get less because they are less popular. We would have a patchwork of services based on popularity and whim rather than obligation."[42] The complaint is offensive in describing contemptuously as *whims* what in fact are the donors' judgments about the use of money they have earned to achieve ends they value. The invidious comparison of private and government programs is also unwarranted.

To be sure, there are fads in private philanthropy, and there is waste. Some charities spend disproportionate amounts of money on fundraising, using the proceeds of one direct-mail campaign to pay for the next one. But there are published standards on fundraising costs that donors can use to compare the organizations soliciting their money, and the better charities far exceed those standards. Government programs, moreover, do not avoid the problem of a "patchwork of services" attributed to the private sector. Despite the existence of hundreds of government programs, some 40 percent of people living below the poverty line receive no government assistance.[43]

Government programs are subject to the political process. Legislative majorities representing diverse interests and viewpoints must come to agreement before any change is possible. Social service bureaucracies are bound by administrative law, which requires complex rules and procedures for carrying out the legislature's intent. Diversity, flexibility, and innovation are the last things one could hope for under such conditions. As is the case with other enterprises run by government, service is slow and unresponsive to customers, wasteful, bureaucratic, and constantly influenced by political considerations. The problems with AFDC, for example, had been clear since the 1960s, and every administration since then had promised reform. But it took 30 years to get the first significant change in the program—the reforms of 1996—and even those are partial.

Private agencies, by contrast, can adapt more quickly to changing circumstances and to feedback about the success or failure of their efforts. They can adopt new ideas about how to provide aid most effectively without having to go through the federal budget process or being bound by administrative law. Because private agencies are separate and independent, each can go its own way, experimenting with new approaches without putting other agencies at risk; there is no need to find a single nationwide approach. The welfare reforms of 1996 gave states much more latitude to adopt different ways of providing benefits to the poor, and the states have already begun experimenting with some new approaches. But "the laboratory of democracy" provided by 50 states cannot compare with the experience to be gained through hundreds of thousands of private agencies, from local shelters and youth programs to nationwide charities.

In addition to the greater freedom that private agencies enjoy, they have a much greater incentive to look for solutions that work. Government programs are funded by taxes, and failure rarely results in a program's being cut; failure is more often used as an argument that more money is required. But a private agency must raise funds from donors who contribute voluntarily. Its donors are customers who want to see results and can take their money or their volunteer time elsewhere if an organization is not producing results.

In short, a private system of charity has all the advantages of a free market over government planning. It is now common knowledge that government planning does not work in the commercial realm. Why would we expect things to be different in the philanthropic realm?

The Promise of Private Aid

Despite the advantages of private over public programs for helping the poor, many people have expressed misgivings. One common argument among theorists is that charity must be government run because it is what economists call a "public good." If Person A wants to see Person B's poverty or suffering relieved, A can obtain that value if someone else helps B no less than if A helps B himself. This is one of the features of a public good: nonpayers aren't excluded from benefiting. Each of us thus has an incentive not to help the poor, in the expectation that others will help them, and if we all act on that incentive no help will be forthcoming. The only way out of that dilemma is collective provision, to which individuals are forced to contribute.

But it is irresponsible to want help given without any corresponding desire to help. Some people do behave that way, but not everyone; despite the logic of the public-goods argument, many people
are moved by the countervailing logic of the old question, What if
everyone did that? In 1995, for example, 68.5 percent of households
contributed to charity, giving an average of $1,017. Nearly half the
adult population (93 million people) did volunteer work. Volunteers
in formal programs gave 15.7 billion hours, or the equivalent of 9.2
million full-time employees, with a value estimated at $201 billion.[44]
The poor, moreover, are not an indivisible pool of suffering that
must be alleviated as a totality. It is individuals who are poor, and
their plight usually makes the strongest claim on family members,
neighbors, and others in the community who know them. A great
deal of private charity is local in nature. In helping a given person
in my community, I may be conferring unintended value on other
community members who know or encounter him, but not on an
entire society. Those other community members, moreover, are more
likely to know me and thus be in a position to exert social pressure
on me to contribute.

But will private, voluntary giving be enough? That is the first
question raised whenever the proposal to privatize charity is put
forward. The large private charities are often the most vehement in
opposing cutbacks in government spending—understandably, since
most of them receive a major portion of their funding from government contracts. "Private charity is built on the foundation of government welfare," argues an official of Catholic Charities USA, which
gets more than half its funds from government. "We can do what
we do because Government provides the basic safety net."[45]

Governments at all levels currently spend about $350 billion on
means-tested programs.[46] Charitable giving by individuals, foundations, and corporations came to $144 billion in 1995, but only about
$12 billion of that was for human services; another $13 billion was
for health, a category that includes some services for the poor.[47]
Offsetting this huge disparity is the fact that many people give much
more in time, as volunteers, than in money. In the category of human
services, the value of volunteer time came to about $17 billion in
1995. Americans also spent 4.6 billion hours doing informal volunteer work—caring for an elderly or disabled person, helping a neighbor—with a value of perhaps $50 billion.[48]

Even so, by the most generous estimates, private giving for the relief of poverty is well under 30 percent of government spending. Since it does not come close to matching government expenditures, how could it possibly replace them? But that hardly counts as an argument against privatization, for three major reasons. The first is that government causes a significant amount of the poverty it aims to relieve. As we have seen, the package of benefits available to poor mothers typically has a higher value than the money they could earn in an entry-level job. A young mother who has grown up in a welfare family and never completed high school or held a job can easily be sidetracked from the working economy by the welfare system. In addition, as we saw in the previous chapter, government regulations such as the minimum wage, occupational licensing, and business restrictions keep the otherwise enterprising poor from helping themselves. Without those barriers to self-reliance, and without the subsidies that undermine the incentives for self-reliance, it stands to reason that many fewer people would be welfare dependents.

Second, a good deal of the money government spends on means-tested programs never reaches the poor. John Goodman of the National Center for Policy Analysis and others, for example, estimated that in 1992 the nonwelfare income of poor people was $94 billion short of the income necessary for them all to live at or above the poverty line. That is less than one-third of the money government spent to lift them out of poverty.[49] The rest goes to the welfare bureaucracy, consultants, and others who administer the system. Of course it would not be possible simply to send that $94 billion to the poor without some administration, nor would that money eliminate poverty. Poverty is more often caused and sustained by behavioral problems than by strictly financial ones. Still, it is hard to believe that the advantages of private over public aid would not produce a considerable savings.

Third, by nationalizing the charity industry, the government has displaced private spending on the poor. The $300 billion that government spends is taken from the private economy. Some portion of that sum would otherwise be spent on goods and services that create new entry-level jobs, providing opportunities for the poor. And some portion would be contributed to charities. Sixty years of AFDC and 30 years of the Great Society programs have produced the expectation that government will provide an adequate safety net for the poor, and people have shifted their charitable giving to religion, the arts, and other areas. Although it is not possible to quantify this "crowding out" effect precisely, or to predict the amount of private giving that would be shifted to aid for the poor if welfare were privatized, historical research has provided a few hints.

In a detailed study of Indianapolis in the 1870s and 1880s, when government aid was reduced as part of a nationwide reaction against "outdoor relief," Stephen T. Ziliak found that private contributions increased by approximately the same amount.[50] Figures from the 1930s are also illuminating. From 1930 to 1932, as the Great Depression deepened, both government and private spending on poverty relief increased sixfold. After Roosevelt's election, government spending continued to increase rapidly as new programs were introduced, but private spending declined rapidly as people assumed that responsibility had been shifted to the government.[51]

At the same time, private charitable organizations shifted their efforts from poverty relief to other goals. At the New York Association for Improving the Condition of the Poor, for example, "Many families formerly cared for by AICP have been turned over completely to public relief departments."[52] Thus it is not surprising that charitable giving today goes predominantly to religion and other objects, with human services receiving a relatively small portion. But there is every reason to believe that the proportions would change if government were not already spending so much in this area.

Conclusion

We do not know with any certainty what the result would be of leaving aid to the poor in private hands. We can't predict what ideas people will come up with to solve the problems they observe. One can certainly find grounds for pessimism. In his study of 19th-century Indianapolis, for example, Ziliack found that replacing government spending with private funds had no effect on the average spell of welfare dependence, nor on the number of people finding jobs and becoming self-supporting. Nevertheless, private agencies can provide aid on a conditional basis rather than as an entitlement, and thus more effectively encourage responsibility. They can draw distinctions on the basis of character and psychology, tailoring the help they provide in ways that the government cannot. They can intervene in the personal lives of recipients in ways that get to the root of problems but would be intrusive violations of freedom if done by government workers. And private agencies can be much more flexible, responsive to changing circumstances, experimental, and diverse than government bureaucracies.

Nor can we predict how much aid would be given in a private system, nor in what forms. Our point of departure, morally speaking, is not the needs of recipients but the generosity of donors. It is the donors who set the terms. Recipients do not own those who support them, and thus do not have a right that must be met, come what may. Those who would privatize poverty relief do not have the burden of showing that all poverty would be dealt with as effectively as it is today by government programs, although the considerations of the previous section make that extremely likely. The burden is on those who support government programs to show why they think the poor are *entitled* on altruistic grounds to the aid they are receiving.

Compassion and generosity are virtues, and the charitable help they prompt us to provide the less fortunate is, for most of us, a part of what it means to live in a civilized society. But compassion, generosity, and charity are not the sum of morality, nor even its core; and they are not duties that create entitlements on the part of recipients. The poor do not own the productive, nor are the latter obliged to sacrifice the pursuit of their own happiness in service to the poor. If individuals are truly ends in themselves, then charity is not a duty but a value we choose to pursue. Each of us has the right to choose what weight charity has among the other values in our lives, instead of having the government decide what proportion of our income to take for that end. And each of us has the right to choose the particular people, projects, or causes we wish to support, instead of having government make that decision for us.

6. Community and Contract

"We're all in this together." That everyday expression of solidarity captures a feeling that has played a major role in popular support for the welfare state. The feeling is that we live as members of a single society, sharing common resources and common goals, and that one of those goals is the well-being of all members. We have a right to expect that if we play by the rules we will not be left behind. If we succeed, it is by the grace of society, and we have an obligation to help those who have been less fortunate. It is the community's responsibility to ensure that none of its members are destitute, deprived of necessary medical care, or left without the means to live a dignified life in their old age. The welfare state is the instrument we have chosen to carry out this collective responsibility.

The appeal to solidarity is the third and last of the basic rationales for the welfare state. In this chapter we will examine its merits.

Communitarianism

Family and Contract

The appeal to solidarity has an obvious emotional resonance, and it's easy to see why politicians take such frequent advantage of it. It is harder to formulate the appeal as an argument that can be evaluated rationally. Indeed, it has been formulated in many different ways, reflecting somewhat different conceptions of the relationship between the individual and society.

In the 1950s, T. H. Marshall, an influential British writer, expressed the idea in terms of an expanded concept of citizenship. The 18th century, he noted, brought the classical rights of liberty, property, and contract, with the free market as a consequence; the 19th century brought expanded political rights to vote and participate in government; and the 20th century brought "social rights" to welfare and other goods. The latter rights were grounded, according to Marshall, in a more intimate connection between individual and society than the classical theorists of rights had conceived, a connection by which the individual was entitled to unconditional support from the community but was also obliged to serve its interests.[1]

The metaphor of a social contract is another way of putting the point. The metaphor reflects the common view of life in society as a kind of "deal": we play by the rules, we do our part to act responsibly, and society will see to it that we do not fail utterly. "Government entitlements," writes a newspaper columnist, "are part of our national agreement about what it means to be an American."[2] The metaphor was implicit in Bill Clinton's 1992 campaign theme of a "New Covenant—a solemn agreement between the people and their government, based not simply on what each of us can take but on what all of us must give to our nation."[3] The term "covenant" is another way of expressing the idea that individuals enjoy a complex set of positive rights and have a complex set of positive obligations to society. In regard to poverty programs, for example, Robert Shapiro explains, "For practical as well as policy reasons, entitlement reform has to be more than simply the latest way of cutting the deficit. What it could and should be is a basic plank in a new covenant of rights and responsibilities, governing the way Americans secure basic social goods." The "rights" in this covenant include guaranteed health care and retirement income; the responsibilities include an honest effort to support oneself by work.[4] In addition to those recent uses, of course, the language of contract has long been employed to describe Social Security as a system in which "contributions" paid in during a person's working life are "invested" to provide for benefits in retirement.

In his major work, *A Theory of Justice*, political theorist John Rawls appealed to a hypothetical social contract in his effort to provide a philosophical rationale for the welfare state. Rawls was concerned with the question of distributive justice: How should social resources such as wealth and power be distributed? How do we determine what fair shares are? His approach was to imagine that everyone in society gathered behind a "veil of ignorance," where they were somehow prevented from knowing their circumstances in life, and even from knowing their talents, needs, interests, and values. An individual would not know whether he was a corporate CEO or an illiterate homeless person. Lacking that knowledge, according to Rawls, people would agree on the principle that differences in income and wealth should be permitted only if and to the extent

120

that they work out to the benefit of "the least advantaged."[5] A market system is acceptable under that principle insofar as the incentives it provides the most productive people lead them to create new jobs, cheaper products, or other benefits for those who are less productive. The pure market system is not acceptable, however, because it provides no guaranteed safety net for people at the bottom. The "difference principle" requires that society tax away some wealth to provide social insurance and relief for poverty.[6]

The family is another metaphor often employed to express the idea of society as a collective enterprise. The family indeed is a paradigm of a community whose members are joined by a strong sense of common purpose along with mutual, unconditional support. In a keynote address to the 1984 Democratic Party convention, then-governor of New York Mario Cuomo said,

> We believe in a single fundamental idea that describes better than most textbooks and any speech I could write what a proper government should be. The idea of family. Mutuality. The sharing of benefits and burdens for the good of all. Feeling one another's pain. Sharing one another's blessings. . . .
>
> We believe we must be the family of America, recognizing that at the heart of the matter we are bound one to another. . . .[7]

Cuomo invoked this metaphor to rally support for welfare state programs benefiting the poor, the homeless, and the elderly as well as the middle class. A decade later, President Clinton's adviser Michael Lerner sounded the same theme: "The new paradigm . . . emphasizes solidarity, mutual aid, social responsibility, and a sense that we are all in it together and that we must all take care of each other as if we were all part of the same family."[8]

Like the contract metaphor, the family metaphor is often used to defend the Social Security program. Since retirees' benefits do not in fact come from the investment of their taxes, but from taxes on current workers, Social Security is a transfer of wealth from one generation to another. The image of the family is commonly invoked to justify the transfer. Defending Social Security as a common social good, for example, Thomas W. Jones, president of the Teachers Insurance and Annuity Association, argues that within families no one calculates exactly what parents owe children and vice versa:

121

"[B]etween parents and children, and among different generations within families, there is almost always an overriding community of interest."[9]

Despite the protean variety of the forms in which it is expressed, the appeal to solidarity rests on a set of philosophical claims that can be isolated and expressed as an argument for the welfare state. And it is an argument distinct from the others we have considered, with a different focus and different assumptions. Its central concept is not freedom, it is not compassion, it is *belonging*. The focus of the argument is not the freedom of those in need but the security and support they may claim because they belong to a common social enterprise. And the obligations it ascribes to those in a position to help are not based solely on altruism as a personal obligation; the obligations are to other people as members of the same community.

The Claims of Community

Henry Maine, the great legal historian of the 19th century, described the historical evolution of society as a progression from status to contract. Throughout most of human history, society was seen as a kind of extended family. The essential relationship among individuals was that of common membership in the group. The individual was born to a status he did not choose, and the needs of society took precedence over his own. But as a member he could call on the group for support, to which he was entitled unconditionally. That model was gradually replaced by the liberal conception of society as an association of individuals for mutual benefit. The essential relationship became one of voluntary contract among people who were equal in status and could act independently of family, clan, or guild. The individual had rights that could not be violated by society; social institutions came to be seen as means to individual ends; the government in particular was a servant of the people. But individuals could expect no unconditional aid from others.

> Starting, as from one terminus of history, from a condition of society in which all the relations of Persons are summed up in the relations of Family, we seem to have moved steadily towards a phase of social order in which all these relations arise from the free agreement of Individuals. . . . [T]he movement of the progressive societies has hitherto been a movement from Status to Contract.[10]

The appeal to solidarity rests, at bottom, on the view that this movement has been carried too far—that too many of the relationships once determined by tradition or custom, by the family or the station in society one was born to, are now matters of individual choice. The society of contract, according to this way of thinking, has turned us into social "atoms"—and atoms in a gaseous state at that, not bound into solid structures with others. People move from place to place, leaving behind the communities—and often the families—in which they grew up. They congregate in cities where they interact only with the friends and colleagues they have chosen and may never meet their neighbors. They select their careers, ways of life, religions, and political loyalties according to personal preference and deliberation rather than carry forward family traditions. They may rise or fall from their family's social class, depending on the success or failure of their own efforts. They marry, divorce, and remarry at will, making and remaking families to suit themselves.

The communitarian view, to give it the name most often used by its current adherents, is that the vast expansion in the scope of individual choice over the last two centuries has tended to dissolve the ties holding society together. That trend has set people adrift, without the social moorings they need. The marketplace is the world of individual choice, where people interact by contract. It is also a world of self-reliance, competition, and trade, where benefits depend on effort and ability and are never guaranteed. But human beings also need the kind of safe and nurturing environment provided by the family. The family is the safety net of unconditional support. It is the little society where relationships are lifelong and unchosen, the place of which Robert Frost said, "when you go there they have to take you in." But families in the literal sense can't do it all, not all the time, not for everyone. We need some measure of the same kind of support in society at large. And that means the restoration of status, the old regime under which everyone was guaranteed a place at the table.

In the economic sphere, as Gaston Rimlinger notes, capitalism brought liberation from feudal constraints, but it also caused the loss of feudal guarantees:

> The liberal capitalist civilization that emerged in the late eighteenth century rejected the traditional protectionism of the old social order. It denied the poor man's claim to a right

> to protection by society; it discarded the concept of paternal
> responsibility of the rich for the poor. In the liberal industry
> state, every man was to be free to pursue his fortune and
> was to be responsible for his success and failure.[11]

The welfare state arose in part as a reaction against that new kind of personal responsibility. As Mary Ann Glendon observes, "The European welfare state is a curious amalgam of modern socialist thought and premodern understandings of the protection that an overlord owed to his dependents."[12]

But what about the liberty rights on which the society of contract is based? An overlord who offers protection will also exercise control over the clients who receive it—whether the overlord is a landed aristocrat in a feudal system or a social service agency in the bureaucracy of a modern welfare state. As we have seen in previous chapters, entitlement programs curtail the freedom both of those receiving benefits and of those who pay for them. Communitarians respond that the claim to freedom is unfounded because the individual is not fully autonomous, not truly a self-made person. We are raised by families, taught by teachers, helped by strangers, inspired by heroes. We inherit the vast pool of knowledge discovered by previous generations, and the culture they have created, and the wealth they have produced. All of this comes to us free. Don't we owe something in return? Are we not obliged to devote a portion of what we have—a portion, even, of what we are—to carrying on the collective enterprise?

Communitarian philosophers claim that the individual is partly constituted, his deepest identity partly shaped, by the unchosen relationships in which he finds himself enmeshed. For the members of a true community, says Michael Sandel, "community describes not just what they *have* as fellow citizens but also what they *are*, not a relationship they choose (as in a voluntary association) but an attachment they discover, not merely an attribute but a constituent of their identity."[13] And that unchosen constituent of our identity carries with it a host of unchosen obligations. As Alasdair MacIntyre puts it,

> I am someone's son or daughter, someone else's cousin or
> uncle; I am a citizen of this or that city, a member of this or
> that guild or profession; I belong to this clan, that tribe, this
> nation. . . . As such, I inherit from the past of my family, my

city, my tribe, my nation, a variety of debts, inheritances, rightful expectations and obligations. These constitute the given of my life, my moral starting point.[14]

In effect, communitarians hold that society *owns* a piece of the individual. None of us truly has "property in our persons" in the sense propounded by John Locke and other classical liberals. The point is made graphically in John Rawls's *Theory of Justice*. When we bargain with each other behind his "veil of ignorance," we do so without knowing who we are. We do not know what degree of success we have had in life, nor even whether we have the talents and character traits that make success possible. That is why Rawls thinks we would agree to the "difference principle," which permits differences in income and other goods only if those differences work to the advantage of the least well-off. The principle is morally justified, in Rawls's view, by the fact that our talents and character traits are not of our own making. They are a matter of genetic endowment and social conditioning, and so the traits a person gets in the lottery of life are a matter of luck. The difference principle, in Rawls's view, represents "an agreement to regard the distribution of natural talents as a common asset."[15] That is to say, the talents and character traits we possess as individuals are not truly or fully ours. They belong in part to society.

The notion that society owns a piece of the individual is reflected on a less theoretical plane in a communitarian proposal regarding organ donation. "Relevant law regarding 'anatomical gifts,' " argues James Lindemann Nelson, "should be revised to allow organs to be routinely removed from all adults who die in circumstances that allow for transplantation." The author explains his rationale as follows:

> ... organ donation should be regarded as a social duty, not as a matter of individual altruism or self-interest.
> ... our organs are not solely our own, either to give, to withhold, or even to sell freely when we no longer need them. Put simply, we owe our organs to needy others when we're done with them, and you can't keep or sell what you already owe.
> ... By coming together and accepting that we have a duty to share our organs (once we no longer need them) with

those in need, we affirm our solidarity with each other in
the face of the many forces that separate us.[16]

Communitarians thus rely on the same collectivist view of human
nature as did the early theorists of the welfare state, the view that
individuals do not exist as such apart from society and thus cannot
claim rights that override the needs of society. Instead, there is a
complex network of rights and obligations that reflects an ever-
shifting balance between the interests of the individual and those
of society. We may call that network a social contract if we wish,
but it is not a contract that the individual is free to accept or reject
on his own.

Thus Will Marshall, president of the Progressive Policy Institute,
advocates a "third way" in contemporary social policy, one that
"rejects the old choice between conservative neglect and liberal entitlements in favor of a new politics of reciprocity, which stresses the
obligations that citizens owe each other and their country."[17] Mary
Ann Glendon praises European constitutions for provisions that
permit individual rights to be limited or suspended in the name of
the public good. She cites with approval a 1970 decision by the West
German Constitutional Court: "The concept of man in the Basic Law
is not that of an isolated, sovereign individual; rather, the Basic Law
resolves the conflict between the individual and the community by
binding the citizen to the community, but without detracting from
his individuality."[18]

Unlike their forebears a century ago, who were primarily concerned with creating new rights to various benefits, communitarians
today have been more concerned about the explosion of entitlements.
Welfare rights, they argue, have been granted in profusion without
corresponding responsibilities. Amitai Etzioni has called for a "moratorium" on the creation of new rights.[19] Communitarians have
insisted that benefits to the poor be conditioned on their taking
responsibility for seeking work, staying in school, and the like. The
idea, as one academic theorist put it, is that "[s]ocial equity is about
more than auditing categories of expenditure. . . . It embodies a give-
and-take between welfare entitlements and the duties of citizenship,
particularly the duty to be self-sufficient."[20]

The concept of responsibility that communitarians are seeking to
restore is quite different from the classical liberal concept associated

with a society of contract. In a society based on the classical rights of life, liberty, and property, the individual is responsible *for* his own life. He is responsible for working to obtain the things he wants. But he is not responsible—that is, answerable—*to* anyone, as long as he respects the rights of others. Welfare rights, by guaranteeing that he will be provided with necessities, remove from the individual some portion of his responsibility for himself. But that protection carries with it, according to communitarians, a responsibility to society, a duty to support and improve himself.

T. H. Marshall argued that, in addition to paying taxes, the primary responsibility attached to social rights is a duty to work.[21] Before capitalism, he noted, work was enforced as a duty under the feudal system. Capitalism removed that duty: individuals were free to decide whether and where to work, motivated only by the desire to gain, not the fear of punishment; but they could not count on support if they did not work. The benefits automatically provided by the welfare state temper the incentive to work, but welfare theorists are coming to realize that the benefits are sustainable only if people make every effort to support themselves. Work must once again become a social duty. "It is no easy matter," Marshall acknowledged, "to revive the sense of the personal obligation to work in a new form in which it is attached to the status of citizenship."[22]

Similarly, in a speech laying out his plan to create a universal right to health care, President Clinton demanded that people take more responsibility for their health—not for their own sake, but as an obligation to society to help keep down heath care costs. "Responsibility also means changing some behaviors in this country that drive up our costs like crazy.... [We] have higher rates of AIDS, of smoking and excessive drinking, of teen pregnancy.... We have to change our ways if we ever really want to be healthy as a people...."[23] The notion of health as a collective asset is made possible only by a collectivist view of the individual and society.

In any case, despite the greater emphasis they place on responsibility, communitarians today still accept the basic idea that those in need have a claim on society, a right that must be honored, in part at least, through government poverty programs. And social insurance programs like Social Security, which cover people at all income levels, are typically defended as an expression of social solidarity. For example, Robert M. Ball, a former Social Security commissioner and an opponent of privatizing the pension system, argues that the program "is based on the premise that we're all in this together, with everyone sharing responsibility for the security of everyone else, present and future."[24]

The basis for the claims that we possess rights to goods from the welfare state, to summarize the third major argument for such rights, is that man is a social animal. The core idea is the idea of belonging— in both senses of that term. We belong to society as its members, and we belong to society as its property. People are shaped by society, their very individuality constituted by the sum of social influences from which their values, beliefs, and character emerge. People are bound up in relationships, many of them unchosen, that give rise to specific rights and obligations. People live in society as members of a collective enterprise, a kind of large-scale family, with a common purpose that includes the well-being of all members and a common claim on the resources of its members. The welfare state is simply the vehicle for pursuing that purpose and exercising that claim.

Individualism

The Moral Primacy of the Individual

The communitarian view of society is starkly at odds with the philosophy of liberal individualism on which the classical rights of liberty are based. As we have seen in previous chapters, the rights of liberty rest on the view of people as *self-movers*, autonomous beings who need the freedom to act on their own judgment, and as *self-owners* who have the moral right to pursue their own happiness, free of unchosen obligations to serve or sacrifice for others. The function of liberty rights is to protect the individual's freedom to act in pursuit of his goals. Because those rights require that relationships among individuals be voluntary, a society founded on them is a society of contract in Henry Maine's sense.

This is not an anti-social creed, as its critics often claim. Individualists do not believe, as Amitai Etzioni alleges, that "individual agents are fully formed and their value preferences in place prior to and outside of any society."[25] Nor do they deny, as Charles Taylor alleges, that "living in society is a necessary condition of the development of rationality, . . . or of becoming a moral agent in the full sense of the term, or of becoming a fully responsible, autonomous being."[26]

But none of this implies that the individual is a perpetual dependent. The fact that a person's knowledge, skills, and values are acquired in the nurturing environment of the family, the neighborhood, and society at large does not imply that he is permanently dependent on those groups for the maintenance of his identity.

The most important asset one acquires, if one is fortunate in upbringing, is precisely the ability to function independently. The central goal in raising children is to prepare them for life as independent adults, capable of thinking for themselves, making their own decisions, supporting themselves, and choosing the relationships they wish to form with others. Parents do manage to achieve that goal with some regularity. As Michael Walzer notes, communitarians waver between two contradictory complaints against liberal individualism. On the one hand, they argue that it presents a false picture of human nature, exaggerating our independence and ignoring our rootedness in concrete relationships and shared values. On the other hand, they complain that people in our individualist culture are all too independent, too mobile, too willing and able to break the bonds that have hitherto joined them with others.[27]

This is not to say that such bonds are a negligible part of adult life. If they are free to do so, people will associate with others in countless ways, from marriage and friendships to neighborhood or civic associations, business partnerships, bowling leagues, support groups, labor unions, corporations, professional societies, investment consortiums, not to mention the many forms of charitable organization we have discussed previously. People will associate with each other on the basis of virtually any shared purpose or characteristic, from religious or philosophical convictions to a passion for tulips. But those are all voluntary forms of community, chosen by each person because they answer his particular needs and interests as an individual. Precisely because they are voluntary, they are expressions of his autonomy, not limitations to it.

Communitarians also misrepresent the debt we owe society for the benefits we have received. Clarity on this moral issue begins with the recognition that there is no such thing as society as a moral agent. There are parents who raise us, teachers who teach us, friends who give us aid and support, inventors who create the products we use, entrepreneurs who create the companies we work for, artists who inspire us with their visions, thinkers who inform us with their insights and discoveries. To parents we owe gratitude and reciprocal support, a profound but still finite debt. To those who benefit us economically we are obliged to honor the terms of trade—no less but also no more. To the great minds who created the knowledge and culture we all inherit, we owe recognition, but their work has long since entered the public domain. At the end of the day, when those obligations have been met, the moral accounts balance, with no amorphous residue left to be claimed by those who want more from us. Can a welfare mother in Des Moines properly claim a share in what I owe my parents? Can a retiree in St. Petersberg claim a share in what I owe to Aristotle, Newton, Shakespeare, and their peers for all they created? Such claims would be absurd.

What is true of spiritual and cultural wealth is also true of economic wealth. If government transfer programs are to be justified by the idea of social solidarity within the community, or by the idea of a social contract among the members of society, we must have some explanation of where each of us gets the prior right to dispose of others' wealth. The common answer is that wealth is a social product.[28] Production is said to be a cooperative, social process: more wealth is produced in a society characterized by trade and the division of labor than in a society of self-sufficient producers. The division of labor means that many people contribute to the final product, and trade means that an even wider circle of people share responsibility for the wealth that is obtained by the producers. Production is so transformed by those relationships, according to this argument, that the group as a whole must be considered the real unit of production and the real source of wealth. At least it is the source of the difference in wealth that exists between a cooperative and a noncooperative society. Therefore society is entitled to transfer wealth among its members.

But the argument is valid only if we regard economic wealth as an anonymous social product in which it is impossible to isolate individual contributions. And that assumption is plainly wrong. The so-called social product is actually a vast array of individual goods and services available on the market. It is certainly possible to know which good or service any individual has helped to produce. And when the product is produced by a group of individuals, as in a firm, it is possible to identify who did what. After all, an employer does not hire workers by whim. A worker is hired because of the anticipated difference his efforts will make to the final product. That fact is acknowledged by theorists like Rawls when they allow that inequalities are acceptable as an incentive for the more productive to work hard, and thus increase the total wealth of a society. To ensure that the incentives are going to the right people, as Robert Nozick has observed, even the collectivist must assume that we can identify the role of individual contributions.[29]

In short, the fact that man is a social animal, that an individual's life is immeasurably enriched by relationships with others, is perfectly consistent with the fact that individuals are self-movers and self-owners. The doctrine that individuals are owned by society, a doctrine taken to its hideous logical conclusion by the totalitarian regimes of this century, is without ethical warrant. Since that doctrine is essential to the communitarian argument for welfare rights, that argument, too, is without merit. We are *not* "all in this together"— not if that catch phrase means we own each other and have the right to use and dispose of each others' wealth, ambition, and ability.

The Society of Contract versus the Social Contract

The communitarian picture of society, moreover, and in particular its picture of the welfare state, is deeply flawed. In point of fact, the welfare state simply does not and cannot function like a giant family, nor like a vast social contract. The differences are important, for they help explain the many failings of the welfare state.

A society of contract is based on the classical rights of liberty. As we have noted many times, those rights protect freedom of action and thus impose on other people only the negative obligation not to interfere with that freedom. It is therefore not difficult for a legal system to guarantee the compatibility of liberty rights among all the people in a society: each person has the right to do what he wills with his person or property so long as he does not use force against the person or property of others.

When people interact with others by contract, they also acquire positive rights and obligations. When I lease a car, I acquire the positive right to use the vehicle and the positive obligation to make the monthly payment. What is true of an isolated transaction is also true of more enduring associations. When I form a business partnership, or join a fraternal organization, or participate in a book-discussion club, I enter into a pattern of positive rights and responsibilities. This is normally the reason people join such groups: they want the right to the benefits available from the association; they are willing to undertake the obligations involved; they gain the security of knowing that others in the group are similarly obliged and that they can count on fellow members in ways they cannot count on strangers. But those rights and obligations are shouldered freely, through the exercise of each person's basic liberty rights as a human being. And the compatibility of those basic rights carries forward to the complex pattern of positive rights and obligations that people acquire by voluntary contract. Because a contract requires the consent of all parties, one person cannot impose positive obligations on another without the latter's consent. And the positive obligations one assumes do not conflict with his basic rights of liberty, because those obligations have been freely undertaken as an exercise of liberty, in exchange for some positive benefit.

Welfare entitlements to income, housing, medical care, and the like are also positive rights, imposing positive obligations on other members of society to provide those goods and services. But these rights are not the result of contract. The welfare state is predicated on the view of goods and services as inherent human rights, on a par with life, liberty, and property. And this guarantees that the system of rights is riddled with conflicts. For example, a person has a right to the income he earns. Someone who siphoned off some portion of another's income through embezzlement or extortion would be engaged in an act of theft. Yet the government must do just that, through coercive taxation, to support welfare clients' right to a minimum income. Similarly, a minimum wage law that aims to secure the "right to a living wage" for some workers violates the freedom of employees to offer to work for lower wages, and it violates the freedom of employers to employ such workers. A health insurance mandate that protects one couple's right to infertility treatments raises the price of insurance, or drives insurers out of the market, depriving other families of the freedom to purchase the more modest coverage they could afford.

In those and countless other ways, welfare rights as a category conflict with liberty rights. The conflict is inevitable because any welfare right imposes on others unchosen positive obligations that, when enforced, deprive those others of their liberty or property. Welfare rights also conflict with each other, and that conflict, too, is inevitable. All the goods and services to which people are said have a right—food, housing, health care, retirement pensions, unemployment insurance—have to be paid for from the same pool of economic wealth in a society. Even if the government taxed away a larger proportion of that wealth, the different welfare rights attributed to different people would make competing claims upon it. No society is wealthy enough to provide safe and comfortable housing for every family *and* a CAT scan for every sick person who needs one *and* a college education for every qualified student *and* the rest of the open-ended list of goods and services that might reasonably be considered needs.

In light of all the conflicts, the state must pick and choose. The government must decide not only the best methods of protecting rights but the very content of the rights it will recognize. We have a right to whatever income the government decides not to take to provide welfare services, and a right to whatever freedom it decides not to curtail for that purpose. We have a right to those welfare goods the government chooses to provide, in the forms and quantities it selects. The result is a fundamental change in the conception of rights. The original conception, enshrined in constitutions and bills of rights, is that a right protects an individual against encroachment and oppression by society. A right is not a privilege that depends on the will of others but a claim that they are obliged to respect. Once welfare rights enter the picture, however, the unavoidable conflicts among rights, and the need for government to choose among them, turn all rights into privileges. T. H. Marshall put the point with admirable clarity:

> Benefits in the form of a service have this further characteristic that the rights of the citizen cannot be precisely defined. The qualitative element is too great. . . . The rate of progress depends on the magnitude of the national resources and their distribution between competing claims. . . . It follows that individual rights must be subordinated to national plans.[30]

In effect, as Tom Palmer notes, "[R]ights are mere dispensations from power, and what is really being asserted is not a more expansive theory of rights at all, but the elimination of rights and their replacement by an obligation to obey, to submit to the welfare state."[31] Communitarians who decry the belligerent assertion of entitlements, who demand that they be balanced with duties, who call for "a give-and-take between welfare entitlements and the duties of citizenship,"[32] are simply acknowledging the impossibility of genuine rights in the welfare state.

The metaphor of the "social contract" is an attempt to soften this blow. It offers the pleasing fiction that we have all agreed to join our fortunes, pool our resources, and appoint the state the arbiter of rival claims on those resources. If that were true, one could argue that we have voluntarily chosen to accept just that package of rights and responsibilities that the arbiter assigns us. But that is, of course, a fiction. An actual contract derives its binding force from consent, from the manifest intent of the contracting parties to be bound by its terms, as evidenced by their overt consent in speech or writing. The "social contract" was never signed or spoken by anyone. It is a theorist's invention to describe what he thinks people *would* agree to if they were wise, rational, fair—that is, if they agreed with him about social policy. Hypothetical consent is not actual consent, and only the latter can bind.

The metaphor of society as a family is, in this respect, a truer model for the reality of a communitarian society. Within a family, if the concepts of rights and obligations are applicable at all, we might say that children have rights to food, shelter, nurture, education, and support, each in accordance with his individual needs, balanced against the needs of other family members; parents have rights to each others' financial and emotional support and the obligation to provide that support to their children; and children have obligations to accept their parents' authority. Families do function in something like the way communitarians envision for society at large. The "rights" of each member are balanced against those of other members, with conflicts resolved by reference to the good of the whole, which everyone has the responsibility of promoting. Each individual has positive rights vis-à-vis other family members, but only those rights compatible with the needs of other members; and those rights are accompanied by unchosen positive obligations.

In another respect, however, a family is so different from a society that any analogy between them is simply untenable. A family is a common enterprise in which members' lives are joined by a commitment to love and support each other. Families share their resources, normally living together as a single household and meeting their needs as a group. Parents know their children intimately and care for them. It is only on the basis of that deeply personal attachment that parents can make decisions about allocating the family's resources, and only on that basis that they can set rules and impose discipline. The citizens of a nation, by contrast, do not know each other personally. They have not agreed to join their lives or share their resources. Lacking knowledge of and personal attachment to each other, they are not in a position to know what is best for their fellows. And as adults they have the right not to be governed as children.

The only society to which the model of the family might conceivably be extended is a primitive tribe or agricultural settlement. But the society we inhabit today is not an intimate or personal association even in that extended sense. It is chiefly an association of strangers. Virtually every activity we perform during the day involves some interaction with people we do not know. The products we buy are assembled from parts made all over the world, by people who do not speak the same languages, do not share the same customs, and have no inclination to sacrifice their interests for ours. We go to the polls to elect political leaders about whom most of us know very little. We place our savings, and thus our futures, in the hands of bankers, insurers, and mutual fund managers whom we have never met and who invest our money in enterprises we have never heard of.

The communitarian attempt to model a contemporary society on the family runs up against two intractable problems that a society of contract avoids: (1) there is no way for society as a whole to achieve consensus about the ends to be pursued; and (2) there is no way for the state, as an agent of society, to allocate resources to those ends in a rational manner.

Choosing Ends. Communitarians advocate a society in which people spend more of their lives pursuing common aims than individual ones. Individualism in the choice and pursuit of goals is the key element in what they describe as "atomism"—and in what they complain of in American society today. Solidarity means that we share common aspirations; that we have a stake in each others' fortunes; that all of us together are responsible for educating children, saving for the future, insuring against risks to our health, and the like. That is, after all, how families function.

But how do we decide which aims to pursue? Communitarians insist that there are universal categories of human goods such as making a living, educating our children, acquiring knowledge, maintaining our health, saving for retirement, enjoying our leisure, enriching our spiritual lives. True enough. But people do not seek the same concrete goods within those categories. They do not pursue those goods in the same way, nor could they, given their different needs and circumstances. They do not rank the categories in the same order of priority. Indeed, people of different moral and religious views do not even accept the same categories of values as legitimate.

Even within a family, of course, there are differences in individual needs, and there are hard choices to make. Piano lessons for one child mean no summer camp for another. Moving to a town with better schools means living in a smaller house. The time parents spend meeting their own needs is time not spent with the children. But people in families know each other intimately. They can work out such conflicts face to face. Strangers can't. Communitarians recognize that their vision depends on the possibility of consensus, but they are wildly overconfident about the possibility of reaching consensus on goals across an entire society.[33]

What actually happens when a society attempts to pursue an open-ended array of goals collectively is that the effort degenerates into political infighting. Interest groups form around competing goals and engage in political struggle for the power to have the state do as they wish. And since, by the very nature of welfare rights, the state is empowered to define the content of all rights and responsibilities, almost nothing is off-limits in this struggle. Except for a few parts of life that are protected by constitutional provisions, any part of life can be subsidized or regulated—guaranteeing that clashes of interest groups will be pervasive and bitter. Health care subsidies and regulations have created conflicts of interest among doctors, insurers, employers, and patients. Interest groups lobby to have their particular health concerns included in mandatory insurance coverage, for which everyone must pay. And the Social Security system has created a simmering generational conflict between the retired people receiving benefits and the younger workers who pay for them.

Moreover, as William Mitchell and Randy Simmons observe in their recent work on the operations of government,

A welfare industry exists, and it consists not only of the aided and potential beneficiaries but of an entire bureaucratic apparatus—both public and private—to deliver services, income, and benefits-in-kind. Nor should we overlook the rent-seeking producers who supply the resources employed by the industry. Whenever food surplus programs, school lunches, and the like are debated in Congress, highly subsidized farmers and their lobbyists are among the conspicuous log-rollers.[34]

The reality of collective decisionmaking is not the easy unanimity that communitarians envision but rather the spectacle of lobbying and legislative deals, political arm-twisting and influence peddling that greets us on the evening news.

A society of contract, based on individual rights, does not generate the same pressure for consensus, nor the same opportunities for power struggles. The function of rights is to allow people to seek their individual purposes in life independently, without needing permission from others. Collisions between people are avoided, not by shared aims, but by general rules, laws, and principles that apply regardless of what one's goals may be. You and I may have different purposes in attending a meeting, but our respect for the common rules of public discussion allows both of us to pursue our aims without interference. Most purchases I make are from sellers who do not share my goals, but that doesn't matter; all we need is the principle that I must pay them the price they want in exchange for the good I want. I trust my banker, not because I know him well enough to be sure he is devoted to my interests, but because we have a contract that the law will enforce evenhandedly.[35]

Even in a society of contract, of course, people will organize to pursue large-scale projects, and power struggles can occur in any organization in which individuals must act in concert for a common goal. They occur in corporations, universities, and civic associations as well as in governments. A voluntary association, however, unlike a government, must compete for the loyalty of members who are free to leave. It has no existence apart from the individuals who make it up and no value to an individual who does not share its aims. Unless the goals of a group inspire commitment, and its leaders inspire trust in their integrity and competence, its members will find other associations that serve their interests better. That makes consensus easier to achieve than in the political realm. Leaders of voluntary organizations have a greater incentive to seek consensus, and, when agreement is impossible, dissenters can go their own way.

Allocating Resources. When people organize to pursue a collective aim, they need some method of reaching decisions about how to define the goal and how best to achieve it. Even if it were possible to achieve consensus across an entire society, an insurmountable problem would remain: the pursuit of a goal requires conscious deliberation, and there are severe limits on what conscious deliberation can accomplish. One important limit is the inability to forecast novelty and creativity. Inventors come up with new products and methods of production, altering an economy in ways that no one— and no committee—could have predicted. Individual artists and thinkers come up with new ideas that alter a culture unpredictably. Everyone loves the idea of innovation, but few love the reality: new ideas strike most people as strange and risky at best, shocking or unworkable at worst. As John Stuart Mill and many other theorists of freedom have argued, innovation tends to flourish only where individuals can pursue their ideas without needing the permission or agreement of the group.

Another limitation on conscious decisionmaking by a group is the amount of relevant information it can handle. In Russia and the other former communist countries, the effort to run an entire economy by command was a failure because the central planners simply could not acquire and integrate all the information necessary to make rational economic decisions. In a market economy, by contrast, individuals pursue their own ends, subject only to the rule that they must deal with each other by voluntary contract. No one makes any decision about how much steel should be produced, or how many people should work as computer programmers. Yet a complex adjustment of supply and demand arises from the incentives each person faces in the market. If not enough steel is being produced, the price will rise and new producers will enter the field. If there are too many computer programmers, salaries and opportunities in that line of work will decline, and some people will seek employment elsewhere.[36]

The same is true of social welfare. To take the most dramatic example: Bill Clinton's proposed health care reform would have brought the entire industry—doctors, hospitals, health insurers, medical schools, and, not least, patients—under the control of a national health board. Health care was a $1 trillion industry at the time, about the size of the entire economy of France, and the Clinton plan was rejected in part because the impossibility of rational central planning was well-known. Planners could not possibly take account of all the diverse needs and preferences of patients, nor of the trade-offs among the various treatments for illness, nor of the diverse local circumstances relevant to local decisions.

Because government cannot plan an entire society rationally, government action typically has unintended consequences—often consequences that are the opposite of those intended. When Aid for Dependent Children (the predecessor of Aid to Families with Dependent Children and today's Temporary Assistance to Needy Families) was created in the 1930s, the intent was to help widows stay home with their children instead of having to work. The unintended consequence was to attract a clientele of unmarried mothers. When Medicare was created in the 1960s, the intent was to help elderly people get the medical care they need. The unintended consequences were to swell the demand for such care and to discourage doctors from waiving their fees for impoverished patients—two factors that led to soaring prices for everyone else's health care. Of course private firms and philanthropic agencies make mistakes, too. But they have no power to force their mistaken approaches on other firms and agencies. In a society of contract, there can be a much greater diversity in ways of dealing with problems, and much more self-correcting experimentation. Governments, by contrast, tend to adopt universal solutions that implicate everyone in a single approach. What urban specialist Jane Jacobs says of cities is true of social welfare in general: "Big bureaucracies can't allow for the diversity and experimentation that are essential to cities. When mistakes are made, they're made everywhere."[37]

Social Security

In the previous chapter, we traced the ill effects of bureaucracy and monopolization on poverty programs. Those factors have equally bad effects on social insurance, and there is no better example than Social Security, the largest single program of the welfare state. In 1996 it consumed $354 billion, nearly a quarter of all federal expenditures.[38] Overall, it currently provides about half of all retirement income in the country, although the proportion varies a great deal by income level: those in the lowest 20 percent of the income distribution are dependent on Social Security for the bulk of their income, while those in the top quintile depend more on private pensions and income from savings.[39] Because of its size, and because of the way the program is structured, Social Security is the most significant embodiment of the idea that "we are all in this together." And it is facing a crisis that will come to a head over the next two decades, a crisis rooted in its history and in its nature as a system of collective provision for retirement.

When it was created in 1935, the Social Security program was intended as a welfare program, to alleviate poverty among the elderly during the Depression. It was designed, however, not as a means-tested poverty program but as a universal scheme of social insurance. There were numerous reasons for that approach, all of them political. One was to help the elderly poor avoid the stigma of welfare, disguising their dependence within a system of universal dependence on government. One of the authors of the Social Security Act, Sen. Walter F. George, (D-Ga.), asserted,

> Social security is not a handout; it is not charity; it is not relief. . . . As an earned right, the individual is eligible to receive his benefit in dignity and self-respect.[40]

Another rationale was paternalistic: the payroll tax introduced to fund the system was a form of enforced "savings," justified by the assumption that even middle-class people who earned enough to provide for their own retirement were too short-sighted to do so.

A third major reason was to ensure political support for the system by giving the vast majority a vested interest in it. As former secretary of health, education, and welfare Wilbur Cohen put it many years later, "[A] program that is only for the poor—one that has nothing in it for the middle income and upper income—is, in the long run, a program the American public won't support."[41] As an added inducement for widespread political support, the architects of the system created a sense of entitlement by describing payroll taxes as "contributions" workers make to their own retirement accounts.[42] In fact, there are no such accounts and no economic relationship between the taxes one pays and the benefits one receives. But as Franklin Roosevelt explained to an adviser:

> I guess you're right on the economics, but those taxes were never a problem of economics. They are politics all the way through. We put those payroll contributions there so as to give the contributors a legal, moral, and political right to collect their pensions. . . . With those taxes in there, no damn politician can ever scrap my Social Security program.[43]

Roosevelt was certainly astute in assessing political reality. The system he devised has earned a reputation as a "third rail," something politicians dare not touch for fear that voters will cast them out into the wilderness of private life. But political reality is a function of peoples' beliefs and expectations. Beyond those beliefs and expectation is *actual* reality—the reality of facts, of numbers, of causes and effects. And that reality is catching up with the system. To understand why and how, one must understand the ways in which Social Security differs from a genuine form of saving for retirement.

In a private pension plan, individuals save a portion of their earnings in a retirement account; that money is invested and earns interest (or capital gains if it is invested in stocks). For most people, the investment gains are a crucial part of providing for future income. Suppose a person saves $200 per month from age 30 to age 65. (Most people have more than that taken in Social Security taxes.) During that period he will put away a total of $84,000. If the money in the account earns 8 percent annually, a conservative expectation for a fund invested in a mix of stocks and bonds, it will grow to more than $450,000 by the time he retires, enough to buy an annuity paying him about $2,200 per month for the rest of his life. If his money earns 12 percent, he will retire with $1.3 million—probably enough to live on the income alone, without touching the principal.

This is the reality that Social Security mimics. Payroll taxes are described as "contributions" paid into a "trust fund" from which "earned" benefits are paid out on retirement. But the description is misleading, if not an outright lie. The taxes paid by current workers are not actually saved and invested; they are used to pay benefits to current retirees. This "pay-as-you-go" system means that the benefits retirees receive do not come from their own savings. Today, Social Security benefits are earned only in the vague sense that retirees once paid something into the system and are now getting

141

something out of it. But those benefits are not earned in the sense of flowing from investment returns over a working lifetime. They flow from the government's ability to take a portion of current workers' income by force.

Thus the Social Security trust fund is not like a private mutual fund, which contains all the money one has put into it, plus investment returns. The trust fund is more like a checking account: money flows in from taxes, money flows out as benefits, and the government tries to keep a positive balance. Currently, the balance is quite large, and growing, due to tax increases in the 1980s that were intended to build up the fund to help pay for the coming retirement of the Baby Boom generation. Nevertheless, it is only a reserve fund, with enough money in it currently to cover just over a year and a half of benefits.[44] Social Security is still a pay-as-you go system, a transfer of money from one generation to another.

And that is the cause of the coming crisis. The number of retirees keeps getting larger in relation to the number of workers supporting them. In 1950 there were 16 workers for every retired person. That ratio is currently 3.3 and falling. The benefits that Social Security must pay out will soon begin rising at an accelerating pace, much faster than the revenues it receives from the payroll tax, as the Baby Boom generation starts retiring. If we look at Social Security finances in isolation from the rest of the federal government, two dates define the scope of the problem. In 2013 tax revenues will fall below expenditures. At that point, Social Security will have to start drawing down the so-called trust fund to pay benefits. In 2032 the trust fund will be exhausted, and some new source of money will have to be found.

But the problem is even worse than that, because we cannot really treat Social Security finances in isolation. By law, the trust fund is invested entirely in government bonds. One part of the government, the Department of the Treasury, takes money from another part, the Social Security Administration, and promises to pay it back with interest. The government is borrowing from itself. And what it does with the borrowed money is spend it—on the military and the courts, on the salaries of government officials, on subsidies to businesses and artists, on welfare checks. The trust fund has not been invested in enterprises that produce income from which the loan can be paid back. The trust fund is not creating wealth on which it can draw in future years. It has been lent to the federal government to conduct its other operations.

In fundamental terms, therefore, what is happening is that payroll taxes currently fund retirement benefits with some money left over to pay for the other functions of government. As this remainder declines, the government will have to increase taxes, or find some other way to borrow money, or cut other spending. What will happen in 2013 is simply that payroll taxes will no longer cover even retirement benefits, so the government will have to continue increasing other taxes, finding other ways to borrow money, or cutting other programs in order to pay the benefits it has promised to retired people. What will happen in 2032 is not that any real fund will be used up but merely that the amount of new money needed to pay benefits will be very large.

In that year, when those who are now in their 30s begin retiring, there will be fewer than two workers paying taxes to support each retiree.[45] If taxes were kept at current levels, tax receipts would fall short of benefits by $800 billion in that year alone, and the shortfall would continue to increase rapidly thereafter. To cover benefits, payroll taxes would have to rise from the currrent 12.4 percent to about 17 percent.[46] The more likely scenario is that benefits will be cut substantially. Altogether, during the period 2010–2060, when Baby Boomers will be collecting benefits, only between two-thirds and three-quarters of the benefits promised under current law can be paid by taxes that remain at current levels.[47]

Even if, by some miracle, no further changes are made in tax and benefit formulas, a young person entering the workforce today and spending his career under the current formulas will get a pretty dismal "return" on his payroll tax "contributions." William Shipman recently calculated that a low-wage worker born in 1970 can expect a monthly Social Security check of $799 (in 1997 dollars). If his payroll taxes were invested instead in a mix of stocks and bonds, he would have enough at retirement to buy an annuity paying $1,431 per month. For an average-wage worker, the difference is even more striking: a Social Security pension of $1,248 versus a private annuity paying $2,863 monthly.[48]

Thus the current problems of Social Security, and the much worse problems that lie ahead, are the result of two politically inspired decisions. The first was to address the problem of old-age poverty through social insurance rather than a poverty program. That guaranteed that any problem in the finances of the system would involve nearly everyone and thus constitute a profound social crisis. As Jane Jacobs put it, when mistakes are made, they're made everywhere. The second decision was to adopt a pay-as-you-go method of financing, which guaranteed that there would indeed be financial problems.

Those political decisions, in turn, were rationalized by the appeal to solidarity, the philosophical meaning of which we have explored in this chapter. The very structure of Social Security assumes that individuals in different generations are bound up in one community and have unchosen obligations to each other, akin to the obligations among parents and children. It assumes that people have positive obligations to support the elderly, and positive rights to be supported in their own retirement years, not because of voluntary contracts they have undertaken but simply because they belong to the same society. It assumes that decisions about basic security in old age can be made collectively, for everyone in society, on the basis of a rationally arrived at consensus. It assumes that wealth is a collective product that can fairly be redistributed among individuals. And it assumes that the individual is not fully an end in himself but that other members of society own a portion of his productive ability and may use and dispose of that portion as they wish.

None of those assumptions can be justified philosophically, at the level of moral principle. And the problems of Social Security are a practical demonstration of how thoroughly those assumptions clash with reality.

The pay-as-you-go system is an evasion of economic reality. The values that Social Security is intended to provide—income during retirement and protection against the economic risk of disability during our working years—require that money set aside now be invested in some productive enterprise creating wealth. The government has assumed that its ability to tax future wealth is as secure a foundation for future income as is the actual creation of wealth. But that is an illusion, since the wealth may not be there to be taxed. If we treated individuals as ends in themselves, not means to the ends of others, if we permitted them to function as self-owners and self-movers, no one would be able to use the force of government to transfer wealth from others to himself. He could provide for future income and current insurance only by saving and investing, and the nation's retirement system would not be facing a crisis.

The coming crisis could have been foreseen long ago and indeed was foreseen by some commentators.[49] The crisis is inherent in the nature of a pay-as-you-go system that is vulnerable to demographic change. It is also unnecessary. A private system of individual retirement accounts, invested in productive enterprises, is not subject to any of the problems facing Social Security. Such private systems have been adopted in varying degrees by other countries that are more far-sighted than we are and have faced the problem of a growing elderly population sooner than we have.[50] To the extent that the retirement system is privatized, it will have three essential features that Social Security lacks, three features essential to a genuine society of contract.

Responsibility. Individuals and families will be responsible for their own future. Those who save money in a private system will have a retirement income; those who do not will not. The frugal will enjoy the fruits of their own efforts; the improvident will suffer the consequences of their own irresponsibility. They will have to rely on charity. That's a hard principle to adopt, and it's harder still to practice. But surely it is a gross travesty of justice to serve the short-term interests of the irresponsible by locking everyone else into a system that sacrifices their well-being.

Responsibility is a matter of cause and effect: the actions one takes now, or fails to take, have consequences for the future. In the current system, there is only the weakest of connections between cause and effect. At the basic level, of course, there is no connection whatever, not in real economic terms. The taxes one pays are not saved and invested for one's own retirement. Each generation is taxed to pay for its elders, in the hope that future generations will submit to taxation for its sake.

Social Security benefit formulas do attempt to create, through law, a correlation between monthly retirement benefits and the wages earned (and thus the taxes paid) during one's working years. But the correlation is weak. For those retiring at any given time, the benefit formulas are skewed to favor low-income workers, who thus receive a higher "return" on their taxes. And the formulas apply to only 35 years of earnings, so that taxes paid during any additional years of work yield no return whatever.

145

There is an even greater variation, however, among people retiring at different points in time. Over the years, Congress has repeatedly increased payroll taxes. It has also repeatedly changed benefits—sometimes increasing them, sometimes trimming them back. As a result, people of different ages will have paid very different amounts of tax by the time they retire and can expect different amounts of total benefits. Over the course of Social Security's history, and for the foreseeable future, the trend has been downward: the later you were born, the lower the return you can expect on your tax dollars. During the early years, when all workers were paying into the system but relatively few retirees qualified for benefits, taxes could be kept low and retirees received much more than they paid. But as the system matured, that windfall disappeared. At the same time, longer life spans and demographic shifts have dramatically increased the burden that retirement benefits place on workers. The combined payroll tax on employees and employers has increased from 2 percent of the first $3,000 of income to 12.4 percent of the first $65,400. In real dollars, taxes increased 900 percent between 1951 and 1995, while benefits increased 188 percent.[51] Today, a couple who are 79 years old and earned the average income during their working years can expect a 17 percent return on their taxes, while an identical couple aged 64 will get a return of only 2 percent, far less than private savings would yield.[52]

Choice. Along with real responsibility for their futures, a private retirement system will give individuals choice, control, and flexibility. Under Social Security, a person begins to "save" for his retirement the moment he starts working, no matter how low a wage he earns. He puts aside the same percentage of his wages every week for the rest of his career, regardless of the financial ups and downs he experiences; and he puts aside exactly the same percentage as everyone else, regardless of differences in circumstances. He is expected to retire at the same age and to draw a pension defined by the same formula. He can neither opt out of the system nor change its terms. In no other part of their lives are people in a free society so regimented.

In a private, voluntary system, people will be as free to choose how to provide for retirement, as they are to choose whom to marry, whether to have children, where to go on vacation, which baseball team to root for. They will be free to decide when to start saving, and how much to put aside in each period of their working lives. One person will start early, to watch the miracle of compound interest work for him; another will put off saving until his middle years, when his income is higher, and meanwhile invest in his education. People will be free to decide what level of income they want in retirement. One person might dream of traveling, and save for the substantial income required; another might want a quieter life requiring less money. People will be free to decide how to invest their savings, according to the level of risk they are comfortable with and the amount of time they want to spend managing their investments. And they will be free to decide how to cash in on their savings when they do retire. One couple may want to live off the interest and leave the principal to their children; another couple, childless, may choose to consume the principal as well and buy an annuity. Why should we not be free to make the decisions that the government now makes about how to use the eighth of our income it takes from us?

Security. A private system, finally, will give people the security of ownership. Their retirement funds will be fully and exclusively their property. The money they save will remain theirs, rather than flow anonymously into the public coffers, with only a tentative promise to show for it.

This is the cruelest illusion that the architects of Social Security created, the illusion that it is merely a government-run savings program through which we "contribute" to accounts that will pay out benefits later. There are no such accounts, nor any property or contractual rights to benefits. As Abram de Swaan observes, Social Security entitlements represent a claim on "transfer capital," the pool of capital that government transfers from taxpayers to beneficiaries. But such entitlements do not constitute genuine property rights.

> [T]he participants in social security cannot dispose of their share in the transfer capital: transfer property is not transferable. They can exert a measure of control only in their capacity of citizens or union members, voters who—in theory—can influence decision-making on social-security taxes, benefits and conditions of payment.

Their diluted control is like that of the shareholders in a corporation. But "shares can be freely bought or sold, savings placed or withdrawn, but the entitlement to social security is not for sale: it constitutes an inalienable right—and an inescapable duty."[53]

The Supreme Court ruled that workers do not have accrued property rights either to the amounts they have paid into the system or to the legislated benefits. Its reasoning was that the notion of payroll taxes as contributions to one's own retirement account can't be taken literally.

> [E]ach worker's benefits, though flowing from the contributions he made to the national economy while actively employed, are not dependent on the degree to which he was called upon to support the system by taxation. It is apparent that the noncontractual interest of an employee covered by the [Social Security] Act cannot be soundly analogized to that of the holder of an annuity, whose right to benefits is bottomed on his contractual premium payments.[54]

The Court upheld the provision of the Social Security Act that states, "The right to alter, amend, or repeal any provision of this Act is hereby reserved to the Congress." The government, in other words, can change the terms of the deal at any time, regardless of how much money one has paid in, and it has done so repeatedly. Tax and benefit levels have frequently been changed. The government has unilaterally decided to tax the benefits of retirees, to eliminate student benefits for which deceased parents had "paid," and to increase the retirement age. No private pension fund or insurance company would be allowed such legerdemain; it would be prosecuted for fraud. The great "social contract" among generations that Social Security is said to represent involves, at its core, the suspension of genuine contractual rights.

In response to questions about the future cost of the Clinton health care proposals, Hillary Rodham Clinton said, "When Franklin Roosevelt proposed Social Security, he didn't go out selling it with actuarial tables. . . . He basically said, 'Look, here's the deal: you pay; you're taken care of; you have social security in your old age.' "[55] This is precisely the problem with Social Security, as it would have been a problem with the Clinton health care plan: the blithe indifference to economic reality, on the assumption that "we're all in this together." And, conversely, the problem with that appeal to solidarity as a moral premise is that it encourages such indifference.

Conclusion

Communitarians advocate a return, at least in part, to a society of status: a pre-modern, pre-liberal conception according to which an individual's relationships to others are not chosen but predetermined or imposed. According to this conception, we look to society rather than our own efforts for our support; we are responsible to society for working and supporting the social good; we belong in part to society, not fully to ourselves.[56] But there is no warrant for this return to pre-modern principles. Our identity as individuals is not so shaped by social influences as to make us perpetual dependents. Our debts to others are not so open-ended as to give them property in our persons. As self-movers and self-owners we have rights to life, liberty, and property, and the social expression of those rights is a society of contract, not status. Henry Maine was right: the society of contract and the society of status reflect two fundamentally opposed principles.

Man is a social animal, and a society of contract is a genuine society. It is chiefly a civil society, a world of commercial enterprise and voluntary noncommercial organizations, with the political sector playing the minimal role of maintaining order and adjudicating disputes about the boundaries of rights. Everything that is true and appealing in the communitarian vision is available in civil society. Freedom breeds a spirit of genuine solidarity among people who independently embrace the same values. It breeds a spirit of responsibility among people who know they cannot draft others, by force, to enroll in their projects.

But nothing in the communitarian vision that goes beyond civil society—nothing that presupposes positive political rights to welfare goods, nothing that requires the state as a primary agent—is either true or appealing, or workable. A modern society does not and cannot function as a giant family, and the effort to make it do so has destructive effects on everyone involved. It breeds a political struggle among interest groups for control of the levers of power. It produces unintended consequences that cannot easily be corrected. And, as the looming crisis of Social Security illustrates so clearly, it encourages people to act irresponsibly in the expectation that others can be forced to clean up the mess.

7. Conclusion

We have examined the nature of welfare rights, their history, and the philosophical case for them. We have examined the arguments for believing in such rights and seen how the many issues they raise play out in the concrete reality of welfare programs. The conclusion can no longer be resisted: the concept of welfare rights is invalid. There is no warrant for claiming rights to food, shelter, and medical care, to income maintenance, child support, and retirement pensions, at taxpayer expense. Such rights cannot be justified by appeal to freedom, to benevolence, or to community. They do not expand but curtail freedom—that of program clients as well as of taxpayers. They make charity compulsory, undermining any genuine benevolence donors might have toward the poor. They replace the voluntary bonds of a society of contract with the coercive power of the state, undermining genuine community. The concept does not provide a valid rationale for the welfare state; it provides a mere rationalization for the coercive transfer of wealth.

If we want a system based on genuine rights, one that promotes genuine human welfare, we should privatize or simply terminate the government programs. In place of "social insurance," the market can provide real and affordable insurance to protect against the risk of illness, accidents, disability, and unemployment. And for retirement, as we saw in the last chapter, private savings instruments provide a much better return than most people can expect from Social Security. At the very least, people should be allowed to opt out of the social insurance programs, forgoing the benefits to which they would otherwise be entitled in exchange for exemption from payroll taxes. A number of plans have been put forward to allow opting out without harming the interests of current retirees.

As for the public aid programs, the welfare reform measures of 1996 were the right first step, though a small one. Cash benefits at least, though not other benefits, were denied entitlement status, and the states were given authority to try different approaches to relieving poverty. For all the reasons discussed in Chapter 5, however, no government programs can achieve the same degree of diversity and flexibility as private ones. More important, however, the coercive "philanthropy" of public aid presupposes that the donors are owned by the recipients. Voluntary philanthropy is the only system compatible with the fact that individuals are ends in themselves.

The welfare state's crisis of legitimacy is real. It is profound. Behind the social crisis of perverse incentives and disabling pathologies, behind the financial crisis of exploding costs, is a moral bankruptcy. The welfare state rests on a false moral foundation. And we can see the outlines of a sound alternative, one that is built on a foundation of real freedom, real benevolence and community.

Some will say, "So what?" As a vast engine for transferring wealth, the welfare state has created enormous vested interests. Lobbies for the elderly will never agree to let Congress cut back Medicare or Social Security benefits. The poverty bureaucrats will fight to the death any major change in the industry that feeds and clothes them. It is naive idealism to think that the lack of a moral justification represents any sort of danger to the welfare state.

Maybe so. But the cynics have been proven wrong time and again, most recently in the collapse of communism. That system was backed by forces much more powerful than lobbies and bureaucratic inertia. The Soviet state had its secret police. It owned all the media; indeed it owned the entire economy. Yet it collapsed when the central sanctifying myth—the myth of a workers' paradise to be created by collective ownership and economic planning—had lost all credibility. The welfare state has likewise been sustained by nothing more than myth, and it is likewise vulnerable to collapse.

Notes

Chapter 1

1. Norman Ornstein, "Roots of 'Entitlements,' and Budget Woes," *New York Times*, December 14, 1993.
2. U.S. Department of Commerce, Bureau of the Census, *Statistical Abstract of the United States, 1997* (Washington: Government Printing Office, 1997), p. 372, Tables 576 and 577. In calculating total social welfare spending, I have excluded veterans' benefits, which may be considered a payment for services rendered by military personnel. I have also excluded public education. Though the latter *is* a form of social welfare spending, the government's role in education evolved separately from its role in the other programs and rests on a somewhat different set of arguments. Education will therefore not be included in this examination of the welfare state.
3. Michael Tanner, "Ending Welfare As We Know It," Cato Institute Policy Analysis no. 212, July 7, 1994, p. 7.
4. U.S. Department of Commerce, Bureau of the Census, *Statistical Abstract of the United States, 1998* (Washington: Government Printing Office, 1998), p. 375, Table 582.
5. Michael Tanner, Stephen Moore, and David Hartman, "The Work vs. Welfare Trade-Off: An Analysis of the Total Level of Welfare Benefits by State," Cato Institute Policy Analysis no. 240, September 19, 1995.
6. Eleanor Baugher and Leatha Lamison-White, *Poverty in the United States, 1995*, Bureau of the Census, Current Population Reports P60-194 (Washington: Government Printing Office, 1996), Table 3.
7. *Sullivan v. Zebley* 493 U.S. 521 (1990).
8. Caroline Weaver, "Welfare Payments to the Disabled: Making America Sick?" *American Enterprise*, January–February 1995, pp. 61–64.
9. Dana Milbank and Christopher Georges, "Oklahoma's Poor Get the Message, Opt Out of the Welfare System," *Wall Street Journal*, February 11, 1997.
10. James P. Weaver, "The Best Care Other People's Money Can Buy," *Wall Street Journal*, November 19, 1992.
11. Steven Hayward and Erik Peterson, "The Medicare Monster," *Reason*, January 1993.
12. *McKnight's Long-Term Care News*, December 1996, p. 3.
13. Baugher and Lamison-White, Table A.
14. U.S. House of Representatives, Committee on Ways and Means, *1996 Green Book: Background Material and Data on Programs within the Jurisdiction of the Committee on Ways and Means* (Washington: Government Printing Office, 1996), Table 1-50.
15. See discussion of Social Security in Chapter 6.
16. Nathan Glazer, *The Limits of Social Policy* (Cambridge, Mass.: Harvard University Press, 1988), p. 58.
17. Irving Kristol, "A Conservative Welfare State," *Wall Street Journal*, June 14, 1993.
18. Mary Ann Glendon, *Rights Talk* (New York: Free Press, 1991), pp. xi, 48.

19. Amitai Etzioni, *The Spirit of Community* (New York: Crown, 1993), pp. 5–9.

20. Charles Murray, *Losing Ground: American Social Policy, 1950–1980* (New York: Basic Books, 1984).

Chapter 2

1. Cf. Martin Diamond, "The Declaration and the Constitution," in *The American Commonwealth*, ed. Nathan Glazer and Irving Kristol (New York: Basic Books, 1976), p. 47:

> for the founding generation it was liberty that was the comprehensive good, the end against which political things had to be measured; and democracy was only a form of government which, like any other form of government, had to prove itself adequately instrumental to the securing of liberty.

2. Allan Bloom, *The Closing of the American Mind* (New York: Simon & Schuster, 1987), p. 27.

3. Robert Green McCloskey, ed., *The Works of James Wilson* (Cambridge, Mass.: Harvard University Press, 1967), vol. 2, p. 585.

4. Louis Henkin, *The Age of Rights* (New York: Columbia University Press, 1990), pp. 101, 153.

5. General Accounting Office, *A Glossary of Terms Used in the Federal Budget Process*, 3d ed. (Washington: GAO, 1981), p. 57.

6. U.S. Senate, *Social Security Amendments of 1970*, Senate Report 91-1431, 91st Cong., 2d sess. (Washington: Government Printing Office, 1970), p. 357.

7. For accounts of the welfare rights movement of this period, see Shep R. Melnick, *Between the Lines: Interpreting Welfare Rights* (Washington: Brookings Institution, 1994); and Martha Davis, *Brutal Need: Lawyers and the Welfare Rights Movement* (New Haven, Conn.: Yale University Press, 1993).

8. *Shapiro v. Thompson*, 394 U.S. 618 (1969).

9. *Goldberg v. Kelly*, 397 U.S. 254, 261 (1970); and Charles Reich, "The New Property," *Yale Law Journal* 73 (1964): 733–87.

10. *Lavine v. Milne*, 424 U.S. 577, 584 n. 9 (1976).

11. *Dandridge v. Williams*, 397 U.S. 471, 487–88 (1970).

12. See Frank I. Michelman, "Welfare Rights in a Constitutional Democracy," *Washington University Law Quarterly*, no. 3 (Summer 1979): 659–93; and Peter B. Edelman, "The Next Century of Our Constitution: Rethinking Our Duty to the Poor," *Hastings Law Journal* 39 (1987): 1–61.

13. Henkin, p. 153.

14. "But the Right to Labor—that is, to constant Employment with a just and full Recompense—cannot be guaranteed to all without a radical change in our Social Economy." Horace Greeley, "The Right to Labor" in *Hints toward Reforms* (New York: Fowlers and Wells, 1855), p. 321.

15. Franklin D. Roosevelt, "Campaign Address on Progressive Government at the Commonwealth Club," San Francisco, September 23, 1932, in *The Public Papers and Addresses of Franklin D. Roosevelt*, vol. 1, *The Genesis of the New Deal* (New York: Random House, 1938), p. 752.

16. Franklin D. Roosevelt, "Annual Message to Congress," January 11, 1944, in *Public Papers and Addresses*, 1944–45 vol., *Victory and the Threshold of Peace* (New York: Harper and Brothers, 1950), p. 41.

17. James W. Nichol, *Making Sense of Human Rights* (Berkeley: University of California Press, 1987), p. 3.

18. Joel Feinberg, *Social Philosophy* (Englewood Cliffs, N.J.: Prentice-Hall, 1973), pp. 58–59.

19. T. H. Marshall, *Citizenship and Social Class* (Cambridge: Cambridge University Press, 1950), pp. 34–35.

20. See Jerome Barron, "Access to the Press—A New First Amendment Right," *Harvard Law Review* 80 (1967): 1641–78.

21. Roosevelt, "Campaign Address on Progressive Government at the Commonwealth Club," p. 749.

22. Edward Sparer, "The Right to Welfare," in *The Rights of Americans*, ed. Norman Dorsen (New York: Pantheon, 1971), p. 82.

23. Adam Smith, *Theory of Moral Sentiments*, ed. D. D. Raphael and A. L. MacFie (1757; Oxford: Clarendon, 1976), p. 82.

24. Daniel Boorstin, *The Lost World of Thomas Jefferson* (New York: H. Holt, 1948), pp. 195–96.

25. Henkin, p. 10.

26. See, for example, Thomas Pogge, *Realizing Rawls* (Ithaca, N.Y.: Cornell University Press, 1989); Charles Beitz, *International Ethics* (Princeton, N.J.: Princeton University Press, 1985); and Paul J. Weithman, "Natural Law, Solidarity, and International Justice," in *Free Movement: Ethical Issues in the Transnational Movement of People and Money*, ed. Brian Barry and Robert E. Goodin (University Park: Pennsylvania State University Press, 1992).

27. See, for example, David Miller, "The Ethical Significance of Nationality," *Ethics* 98 (1988): 647–62.

28. See Stephen Holmes, *Passions and Constraint: On the Theory of Liberal Democracy* (Chicago: University of Chicago Press, 1995); and Jeremy Waldron, *'Nonsense upon Stilts': Bentham, Burke, and Marx on the Rights of Man* (London: Methuen, 1987), p. 157.

29. Thomas Buergenthal, "To Respect and to Ensure: State Obligations and Permissible Derogations," in *The International Bill of Rights*, ed. Louis Henkin (New York: Columbia University Press, 1981), p. 77.

30. *DeShaney v. Winnebago County Department of Social Services*, 489 U.S. 196, 201 (1989).

31. U.S. Department of Commerce, *Statistical Abstract of the United States, 1997* (Washington: Government Printing Office, 1997), Tables 576, 338, 515.

32. D. D. Raphael, "Human Rights, Old and New," in *Political Theory and the Rights of Man*, ed. D. D. Raphael (Bloomington: Indiana University Press, 1967).

Chapter 3

1. Friedrich Engels, *The Condition of the Working Class in England*, trans. and ed. W. O. Henderson and W. H. Chaloner (Oxford: Basil Blackwell, 1958), pp. 10, 12.

2. Phyllis Deane, *The First Industrial Revolution* (Cambridge: Cambridge University Press, 1965), p. 21. See also T. S. Ashton, *The Industrial Revolution: 1760–1830*, rev. ed. (Oxford: Oxford University Press, 1962), p. 100.

3. E. A. Wrigley and R. S. Schofield, *The Population History of England 1541–1871* (Cambridge, Mass.: Harvard University Press, 1981), chap. 10.

4. F. A. Hayek, "History and Politics," in *Capitalism and the Historians*, ed. F. A. Hayek (Chicago: University of Chicago Press, 1954), p. 16.

5. Deane, p. 266.
6. Wrigley and Schofield, p. 412.
7. Gertrude Himmelfarb, *Poverty and Compassion* (New York: Vintage Books, 1992), p. 25 ff.
8. Willford Isbell King, *The Wealth and Income of the People of the United States* (New York: Macmillan, 1917), pp. 128–30.
9. Alexis de Tocqueville, "Memoir on Pauperism," in *Tocqueville and Beaumont on Social Reform*, ed. and trans. Seymour Drescher (New York: Harper & Row, 1968), p. 10.
10. J. A. Hobson, *Problems of Poverty: An Inquiry into the Industrial Condition of the Poor* (1891; New York: Augustus M. Kelley, 1971), p. 28.
11. Gertrude Himmelfarb, *The De-moralization of Society* (New York: Alfred A. Knopf, 1995), p. 130.
12. Tocqueville, p. 19.
13. *Poor Law Commissioners Report of 1834* (London: Darling & Son, 1905), p. 228.
14. Ibid., p. 264.
15. Himmelfarb, *The De-moralization of Society*, p. 137; and Geoffrey Best, *Mid-Victorian Britain* (New York: Schocken Books, 1972), p. 140.
16. Walter I. Trattner, *From Poor Law to the Welfare State: A History of Social Welfare in America* (New York: Free Press, 1974), pp. 55–56. See also Raymond A. Mohl, "Three Centuries of American Public Welfare: 1600–1932," *Current History*, July 1973, p. 6.
17. Franklin Pierce, "Veto Message," May 3, 1854, in *A Compilation of the Messages and Papers of the Presidents* (New York: Bureau of National Literature, 1897), vol. 7, pp. 2781, 2782.
18. Marvin Olasky, *The Tragedy of American Compassion* (Washington: Regnery, 1992), p. 58.
19. Best, pp. 138, 145.
20. Charles Richmond Henderson, *Modern Methods of Charity* (New York: Macmillan, 1904), pp. 447–48.
21. Paul Starr, *The Transformation of American Medicine* (New York: Basic Books, 1982), p. 182.
22. Charles Loch Mowat, *The Charity Organisation Society: 1869–1912, Its Ideas and Work* (London: Methuen, 1961), p. 58.
23. Quoted in ibid., p. 72.
24. Mary E. Richmond, *Friendly Visiting among the Poor: A Handbook for Charity Workers* (New York: Macmillan, 1916), p. 151.
25. Mohl, pp. 8–9.
26. See David G. Green, *Reinventing Civil Society: The Rediscovery of Welfare without Politics* (London: Institute for Economic Affairs, Health and Welfare Unit, 1993), p. 56.
27. See Starr, p. 206. David T. Beito estimates that, around 1920, 30 percent of adult men were members. David T. Beito, "Lodge Doctors and the Poor," *The Freeman*, May 1994, p. 220. Alvin J. Schmidt cites an estimate of 50 percent of the entire population in *Fraternal Organizations* (Westport, Conn.: Greenwood, 1980), p. 1.
28. Robert E. Park and Herbert A. Miller, *Old World Traits Transplanted* (New York: Harper & Brothers, 1921), p. 129.
29. Abram de Swaan, *In Care of the State: Health Care, Education and Welfare in Europe and the USA in the Modern Era* (New York: Oxford University Press, 1988), chap. 5.
30. Carolyn Weaver, "On the Lack of a Political Market for Compulsory Old-Age Insurance prior to the Great Depression," *Explorations in Economic History* 20 (1983): 311.

31. Daniel Levine, *Poverty and Society* (New Brunswick, N.J.: Rutgers University Press, 1988), pp. 54–55.

32. Speech of May 18, 1889, quoted in Gaston V. Rimlinger, *Welfare Policy and Industrialization in Europe, America, and Russia* (New York: John Wiley & Sons, 1971), p. 121.

33. Rimlinger, p. 87. See also Ralph Raico, "The Rise of the Modern Welfare State and the Liberal Response," in *Studien zur Geschichte des deutschen Liberalismus*, ed. Ralph Raico (Cologne: Institut für Wirtshaftspolitik, 1998).

34. Quoted in Bentley B. Gilbert, *The Evolution of National Insurance in Great Britain* (London: Michael Joseph, 1966), p. 253.

35. Henry R. Seager, *Social Insurance* (New York: Macmillan, 1910); and Irving R. Rubinow, *Social Insurance* (New York: Henry Holt, 1916).

36. Theda Skocpol, *Protecting Soldiers and Mothers* (Cambridge, Mass.: Harvard University Press, 1992), pp. 132, 149, 156.

37. Quoted in Rimlinger, pp. 76, 77–78.

38. Skocpol, chaps. 8–9.

39. de Swaan, p. 179.

40. Ibid., p. 189.

41. Green, p. 31.

42. W. Michael Cox and Richard Alm, "The Good Old Days Are Now," *Reason*, December 1995, p. 24.

43. Gilbert, p. 170 ff.

44. Exact estimates vary. See Rimlinger, p. 194 ff; de Swaan, p. 205; Weaver, p. 314; and W. Andrew Achenbaum, *Social Security: Visions and Revisions* (New York: Cambridge University Press, 1986), p. 15.

45. Gilbert, p. 265.

46. Rimlinger, p. 194.

47. Michael Rappaport, "The Private Provision of Unemployment Insurance," *Wisconsin Law Review* 61 (1992): 68.

48. See, for example, Richard Ely, *Social Aspects of Christianity and Other Essays* (New York: T. Y. Crowell, 1889). "Coercive philanthropy is philanthropy of governments, either local, state, or national. The exercise of philanthropy is coming to an increasing extent to be regarded as the duty of government" (p. 92).

49. Olasky, chap. 8.

50. That was one reason the friendly societies in England fought against the social insurance programs: they saw that money taken for taxes would be money not available for workmen to use as membership fees in the voluntary societies. See Bentley, p. 160 ff.

51. de Swaan, p. 188. See also Raico.

52. Indeed, reformers like Frank Dekker Watson, director of the Pennsylvania School for Social Service, argued that private charity should be actively discouraged because it stood in the way of the growth of government. See Frank Dekker Watson, *The Charity Organization Movement in the United States* (New York: Macmillan, 1922), pp. 398–99. See also Norman Furniss and Timothy Tilton, *The Case for the Welfare State* (Bloomington: Indiana University Press, 1977). "Constitutional considerations aside, advocates of social reform, in comparison to their counterparts in Europe, had to deal with a far more complex social structure that provided, in an ad hoc manner, major nongovernmental forms of relief from individual destitution" (p. 155).

53. Gilbert, p. 450.

54. R. H. Tawney, *The Acquisitive Society* (New York: Harcourt, Brace and Howe, 1920), p. 3.

55. James Wilson, "Of the Natural Rights of Individuals," in *The Works of James Wilson*, ed. Robert Green McCloskey (Cambridge, Mass.: Harvard University Press, 1967), vol. 2, pp. 241–42.

56. See John Locke, *Second Treatise on Civil Government*, chap. 9; and William Blackstone, *Commentaries on the Laws of England*, book I, sec. 1.

57. See Nassau W. Senior, *Historical and Philosophical Essays* (London: Longman, Green, Longman, Roberts, and Green, 1865), vol. 2, p. 115.

58. William Graham Sumner, *What the Social Classes Owe to Each Other* (1883; Caldwell, Idaho: Caxton, 1974), p. 24.

59. See Joyce Appleby, *Capitalism and a New Social Order: The Republican Vision of the 1790s* (New York: New York University Press, 1984). "The old formulation had said that only some people were capable of rational behavior and that they should be entrusted with authority to direct others. The modern concept of self-interest gave to all men the capacity for rational decisions directed to personal ends. . . . Jeffersonian Republicans seized upon the liberating potential in this new conception of human nature and invested self-interest with moral value. Self-interest—reconceived— turned out to be a mighty leveller, raising ordinary people to the level of competence and autonomy while reducing the rich, the able, and the well-born to equality" (p. 97).

60. Scholars have debated the extent of this individualism and the degree of influence of its chief philosophical exponent, John Locke, on the American Founders. For a summary of the current consensus, which recognizes that Lockean individualism indeed played a major role, see Jerome Huyler, *Locke in America: The Moral Philosophy of the Founding Era* (Lawrence: University Press of Kansas, 1995), pp. 1–29.

61. In an early essay, Marx complained, "None of the so-called rights of man goes beyond egoistic man, man as he is in civil society, namely an individual withdrawn behind his private interests and whims and separated from the community." Karl Marx, "On the Jewish Question," in *Karl Marx Early Texts*, trans. and ed. David McLellan (Oxford: Basil Blackwell, 1971), p. 104.

62. J. A. Hobson, *The Crisis of Liberalism* (1909; Hassocks, England.: Harvester, 1974), p. 113.

63. Louis B. Brandeis, "Workingmen's Insurance—The Road to Social Efficiency," in *Proceedings of the National Council of Charities and Correction*, ed. Alexander Johnson (Fort Wayne, Ind.: Fort Wayne Printing, 1911), p. 157. See also John Dewey, *Liberalism and Social Action* (New York: Capricorn Books, 1935), p. 27.

64. "Annual Message to Congress," January 6, 1941, in Franklin D. Roosevelt, *The Public Papers and Addresses*, 1940 vol., *War and Aid to Democracies* (New York: Macmillan, 1941), p. 672. Three years later, in his state of the union address, he told Congress, "We have come to a clear realization that individual freedom cannot exist without economic security and independence. 'Necessitous men are not free men.' " "Annual Message to Congress," January 11, 1944, in Franklin D. Roosevelt, *The Public Papers and Addresses*, 1944–45 vol., *Victory and the Threshold of Peace* (New York: Harper & Brothers, 1950), p. 41.

65. Herbert Samuel, *Liberalism: An Attempt to State the Principles and Proposals of Contemporary Liberalism in Britain* (London: G. Richards, 1902), p. 26. See also L. T. Hobhouse, *Liberalism* (Oxford: Oxford University Press, 1964), pp. 49–50.

66. Dewey, *Liberalism and Social Action*, p. 63.

67. "Campaign Address on Progressive Government at the Commonwealth Club," San Francisco, September 23, 1932, in Franklin D. Roosevelt, *The Public Papers and Addresses*, vol. 1, *The Genesis of the New Deal* (New York: Random House, 1938), p. 749.

68. Hobhouse, p. 78.

69. Norman Barry, *Welfare* (Minneapolis: University of Minnesota Press, 1990), p. 34.

70. Speech on the third anniversary of the Social Security Act, August 15, 1938, in Franklin D. Roosevelt, *The Public Papers and Addresses*, 1938 vol., *The Continuing Struggle for Liberalism* (New York: Macmillan, 1941), pp. 478–79.

71. Himmelfarb, *Poverty and Compassion*, p. 102.

72. Francis C. Montague, *The Limits of Individual Liberty* (London: Rivingtons, 1885), pp. 57, 147.

73. John Dewey, *Individualism Old and New* (1929; reprint, New York: Capricorn Books, 1962), p. 53.

74. Hobson, *The Crisis of Liberalism*, p. 207 ff.

75. See, for example, Elizabeth Wickenden and Winifred Bell, *Public Welfare: Time for a Change* (New York: New School of Social Work of Columbia University, 1961), pp. 25–27.

76. Owen Lovejoy, "The Faith of a Social Worker," *Survey*, May 8, 1920, p. 210.

77. See Olasky, chaps. 2–5, for a survey of these philanthropists.

78. Rev. R. M. Newton, in *New York Journal*, December 24, 1899, p. 39; cited in Olansky, p. 136.

79. T. H. Green, "Essay on Christian Dogma," in *The Works of Thomas Hill Green*, ed. R. L. Nettleship (1906; reprint, New York: Kraus Reprint Co., 1969), p. 184. See also W. H. Greenleaf, *The British Political Tradition*, vol. 2, *The Ideological Heritage* (London: Methuen, 1983), p. 126.

80. A personal statement of faith, written in August 1883, quoted in Himmelfarb, *Poverty and Compassion*, p. 83.

81. Beatrice Webb, *My Apprenticeship* (London: Longmans, Green, 1926), p. 138.

82. Sidney Webb, "The Difficulties of Individualism," in *Socialism and Individualism*, ed. Sidney Webb et al., Fabian Socialist Series no. 3 (London: Fifield, 1908), pp. 8–9.

83. Alice Raven, "Normal and Abnormal Psychology in Relation to Social Welfare," *Sociological Review* 21, no. 2 (1929): 125. See also Jose Harris, "Political Thought and the Welfare State 1870–1940: An Intellectual Framework for British Social Policy," *Past and Present*, no. 135 (May 1992).

84. Rimlinger, p. 68.

85. Ibid., p. 60; and Starr, p. 193.

86. E. Ainscow, "State and Parent: A Co-operative Partnership," *Social Welfare* 2 (1934): 99–103, quoted in Jose Harris, "Political Thought and the Welfare State 1870–1940: An Intellectual Framework for British Social Policy," *Past and Present*, no. 135, (May 1992): 139.

87. Thomas Paine, *Common Sense*, in *The Complete Writings of Thomas Paine*, ed. Philip S. Foner (New York: Citadel, 1945), vol. 1, p. 4.

88. Montague, p. 149.

89. The Earl of Oxford and Asquith [Herbert H. Asquith], *Memories and Reflections 1852–1927* (Boston: Little, Brown, and Company, 1928), vol. 1, p. 135.

90. "Annual Message to Congress," January 3, 1936, in Franklin D. Roosevelt, *The Public Papers and Addresses*, vol. 5, *The People Approve* (New York: Random House, 1936), p. 13.

91. Herbert Spencer, *The Man versus the State* (1884; Indianapolis: Liberty Classics, 1982), p. 46.

92. Cass Sunstein, "Constitutionalism after the New Deal," *Harvard Law Review* 101 (1987): 422 ff.

93. See, for example, Dewey, *Liberalism and Social Action*, p. 73 ff; and Dewey, *Individualism Old and New*, p. 93 ff.

94. Barry, p. 34.

95. Roosevelt, *Public Papers and Addresses*, 1944–45 vol., p. 41.

96. In his first campaign for the presidency, he told an audience, "As I see it, the task of Government in its relation to business is to assist the development of an economic declaration of rights, an economic constitutional order." Roosevelt, *Public Papers and Addresses*, vol. 1, p. 752.

97. Himmelfarb, *Poverty and Compassion*, p. 204.

98. Stefan Collini, *Liberalism and Sociology: L. T. Hobhouse and Political Argument in England, 1880–1914* (Cambridge: Cambridge University Press, 1979), p. 134.

99. Rimlinger, p. 229.

Chapter 4

1. Norman Furniss and Timothy Tilton, *The Case for the Welfare State: From Social Security to Social Equality* (Bloomington: Indiana University Press, 1977), p. 31.

2. *Rothstein v. Wyman*, 303 F. Supp. 339, 346–47 (1969) (rev. 467 F.2d 226 (1972)).

3. Franklin D. Roosevelt, "Annual Message to Congress," January 11, 1944, in *The Public Papers and Addresses*, 1944–45 vol., *Victory and the Threshold of Peace* (New York: Harper & Brothers, 1950), p. 41.

4. F. A. Hayek, *Constitution of Liberty* (Chicago: Henry Regnery, 1960), p. 17.

5. Gerald MacCallum, "Negative and Positive Freedom," *Philosophical Review* 76 (1967): 314, 318–21.

6. Wendy E. Parmet, "Health Care and the Constitution: Public Health and the Role of the State in the Framing Era," *Hastings Constitutional Law Quarterly* 20, no. 2 (Winter 1993): 278.

7. Andrew Levine, "Fairness to Idleness: Is There a Right Not to Work?" *Economics and Philosophy* 11 (1995): 262.

8. Quoted in Robert Pear, "House Takes Up Legislation to Dismantle Social Programs," *New York Times*, March 22, 1995.

9. *Harris v. McRae*, 448 U.S. 297, 316 (1980). See also *Rust v. Sullivan*, 500 U.S. 201 (1991).

10. Philippe van Parijis, *Real Freedom for All* (Oxford: Oxford University Press, 1995), p. 22.

11. John Kenneth Galbraith, *The New Industrial State* (New York: New American Library, 1967), p. 141.

12. Cf. George Reisman, *Capitalism: A Treatise on Economics* (Ottawa, Ill.: Jameson Books, 1996), p. 331.

13. Charles Murray, *Losing Ground: American Social Policy, 1950–1980* (New York: Basic Books, 1984), p. 29.

14. Martina Shea, Bureau of the Census, *Dynamics of Economic Well-Being: Poverty 1990–1992*, Current Population Reports, Household Economic Studies P70-42 (Washington: Government Printing Office, 1995), pp. 2–3, 9–10.

15. Michael Tanner, *The End of Welfare: Fighting Poverty in the Civil Society* (Washington: Cato Institute, 1996), p. 17 ff.

16. M. Anne Hill and June O'Neill, *Underclass Behaviors in the United States: Measurement and Analysis of Determinants* (New York: Baruch College, Center for the Study of Business and Government, August 1993), chap. 2.

17. U.S. Department of Commerce, Bureau of the Census, *Poverty in the United States: 1992*, Current Population Reports P60-185 (Washington: Government Printing Office, 1993), Table 11.

18. Hill and O'Neill, chap. 2.

19. Eleanor Baugher and Leatha Lamison-White, Bureau of the Census, *Poverty in the United States: 1995*, Current Population Reports P60-194 (Washington: Government Printing Office, 1996), Table 3.

20. Mary Jo Bane and David Ellwood, *Welfare Realities: From Rhetoric to Reform* (Cambridge, Mass.: Harvard University Press, 1994), p. 55.

21. Douglas J. Besharov and Karen N. Gardiner, "Teen Sex," *American Enterprise*, January–February 1993, pp. 56–57.

22. William Julius Wilson, *When Work Disappears* (New York: Alfred A. Knopf, 1996).

23. U.S. Department of Commerce, *Statistical Abstract of the United States: 1996* (Washington: Government Printing Office, 1997), p. 404, Table 636; data from Bureau of Labor Statistics.

24. Richard B. Freeman and Harry J. Holzer, "Young Blacks and Jobs—What We Now Know," *Public Interest* 78 (Winter 1985): 27. See also Myron Magnet, *The Dream and the Nightmare* (New York: William Morrow, 1993), p. 47; and Tanner, pp. 19–23.

25. W. Michael Cox and Richard Alm, "By Our Own Bootstraps: Economic Opportunity and the Dynamics of Income Distribution," Federal Reserve Bank of Dallas, *Annual Report*, 1995, p. 8.

26. See U.S. Department of the Treasury, Office of Tax Analysis, "Household Income during the 1980s: A Statistical Assessment Based on Tax Return Data," June 1, 1992; and Isabel V. Sawhill and Mark Condon, "Is U.S. Income Inequality Really Growing?" Urban Institute Policy Bites no. 13, Washington, June 1992.

27. Tanner, p. 169. See also Thomas D. Hopkins, "Profiles of Regulatory Costs," Report to U.S. Small Business Administration, November 1995.

28. S. David Young, *The Rule of Experts: Occupational Licensing in America* (Washington: Cato Institute, 1987).

29. William H. Mellor, *Is New York City Killing Entrepreneurship?* (Washington: Institute for Justice, 1996).

30. Neil Gilbert, *Welfare Justice: Restoring Social Equity* (New Haven, Conn.: Yale University Press, 1995), p. 144.

31. A Roper poll in February 1988 asked respondents to give their opinion on whether something was "a privilege that a person should have to earn, or a right to which he is entitled as a citizen." The results were as follows:

	Privilege	Right
Adequate medical care	26%	71%
Adequate provision for retirement	39%	56%
Adequate standard of living	46%	50%
Basic telephone service	60%	34%
College education	67%	30%

Public Opinion, November–December 1988.

32. David G. Green, *Reinventing Civil Society: The Redicovery of Welfare without Politics* (London: Institute for Economic Affairs, Health and Welfare Unit, 1993), p. 70 ff; and Paul Starr, *The Social Transformation of American Medicine* (New York: Basic Books, 1982), p. 182 ff.

33. For example, an employer might provide a policy costing $4,000; this benefit is not taxed as income to the employee, and the business deducts it as a labor cost. To purchase that same policy with after-tax dollars, a self-employed person would currently have to earn over $7,000, and someone working for a small business without health insurance benefits would have to earn over $8,000. Tanner, p. 170.

34. U.S. Department of Commerce, *Statistical Abstract of the United States: 1996,* p. 112, Table 155.

35. Ibid., p. 483, Table 745.

36. Karen Davis and Cathy Schoen, *Health and the War on Poverty* (Washington: Brookings Institution, 1978), pp. 40–48.

37. John C. Goodman and Gerald L. Musgrave, *Patient Power: Solving America's Health Care Crisis* (Washington: Cato Institute, 1992), p. 232.

38. Stan Liebowitz, "Why Health Care Costs Too Much," Cato Policy Analysis no. 211, June 23, 1994, p. 15.

39. "Less Health Care Seen as Possible," *New York Times,* March 3, 1993.

40. General Accounting Office, "Health Insurance Portability and Accountability Act of 1996: Early Implementation Concerns," GAO/HEHS-97-200R, 1997.

41. Hilary Stout, "Community-Rated Health Plans Prove Popular, but Success May Depend on Universal Coverage," *Wall Street Journal,* June 15, 1994.

42. Merrill Matthews Jr., "Explaining the Growing Number of Uninsured," Brief Analysis no. 251, National Center for Policy Analysis, Dallas, 1998.

43. Quoted in Stout.

Chapter 5

1. "The Quality of Mercy in 1995," editorial, *New York Times,* January 1, 1995.

2. See, for example, Jeremy Waldron, *'Nonsense upon Stilts': Bentham, Burke, and Marx on the Rights of Man* (London: Methuen, 1987). "Humans have other needs [besides freedom], related to their health, survival, culture, education and ability to work.... Some theorists have made this concession through recognizing that the satisfaction of these needs is involved in any genuine concern about freedom. But whether one takes this 'positive freedom' approach or not, it is now widely (though not universally) accepted that material needs generate moral imperatives.... If we want a catalogue of what people owe each other as a matter of moral priority, we should look not only to liberty but also to the elementary conditions of material well-being" (p. 157).

3. Colman McCarthy, "Maia's Choice," *Washington Post,* June 24, 1995.

4. John B. Judis, "Crosses to Bear," *New Republic,* September 12, 1994, p. 25.

5. Peter Wehner, "In Pursuit of Wealth, Christians Have Forgotten Biblical Teachings," *Philadelphia Inquirer,* March 15, 1997, p. A15.

6. Alex Michalos, *The Society for Business Ethics Newsletter* 5, no. 1 (1994).

7. Dennis Kelly, "Students Contest Civic Duty Mandates," *USA Today,* April 19, 1994.

8. Tracy Thompson, "The Wizard of Prozac," *Readers Digest,* October 1994, p. 77.

9. Cf. Ayn Rand, *Atlas Shrugged* (1957; New York: Dutton Books, 1992), p. 1031.

10. See, for a treatment of the virtue of generosity, Tibor Machan, *Generosity: Virtue in Civil Society* (Washington: Cato Institute, 1998).

11. Ayn Rand, *The Fountainhead* (1943; New York: Scribner, 1986), p. 712.

12. See, for example, National Conference of Catholic Bishops, *Economic Justice for All: Pastoral Letter on Catholic Social Teaching* (Washington: United States Catholic Conference, 1986). "Decisions [about our economic future] must be judged in light of what they do *for* the poor, what they do *to* the poor, and what they enable the poor to do *for themselves*. The fundamental criterion for all economic decisions, policies, and institutions is this: they must be at the service of *all people, especially the poor*" (p. 12).

13. Jeremy Waldron, "Welfare and the Images of Charity," in *Liberal Rights* (Cambridge: Cambridge University Press, 1993), p. 225.

14. Robert Nozick, *Anarchy, State, and Utopia* (New York: Basic Books, 1974), pp. 169–72.

15. Richard J. Arneson, "Property Rights in Persons," *Social Philosophy & Policy* 9, no. 1 (1992): 204–5, 207.

16. Rodney Peffer, "A Defense of Rights to Well-Being," *Philosophy & Public Affairs* 8 (1978): 74–75.

17. Ayn Rand, "Faith and Force: The Destroyers of the Modern World," in *Philosophy: Who Needs It* (New York: Penguin Books, 1984), p. 61.

18. Alexis de Tocqueville, "Memoir on Pauperism," in *Tocqueville and Beaumont on Social Reform*, ed. and trans. Seymour Drescher (New York: Harper & Row, 1968), p. 15.

19. Quoted in Nathan I. Higgins, *Protestants against Poverty: Boston's Charities, 1870–1900* (Westport, Conn.: Greenwood, 1971), p. 25, which is quoted in Marvin Olasky, *The Tragedy of American Compassion* (Washington: Regnery, 1992), p. 44.

20. Ibid., p. 75.

21. Robert Moffitt, "Incentive Effects of the U.S. Welfare System: A Review," *Journal of Economic Literature* 30 (1992): 7, 16.

22. For an inside view of those indignities, see Theresa Funiciello, *Tyranny of Kindness* (New York: Atlantic Monthly Press, 1993).

23. Donald Howard, *The WPA and Federal Relief Policy* (New York: Russell Sage, 1943), p. 828.

24. Quoted in R. Shep Melnick, *Between the Lines: Interpreting Welfare Rights* (Washington: Brookings Institution, 1994), p. 86.

25. Robert E. Thompson, *Manual for Visitors among the Poor* (Philadelphia: Lippincott, 1879), pp. 240–41, quoted in Olasky, p. 129.

26. Michael Janofsky, "Kool-Aid, Not Soda: Living on Food Stamps," *New York Times*, April 5, 1995.

27. Steven Greenhouse, "Unions Unite Old Friends in Bashing Their Foes," *New York Times*, November 22, 1996.

28. Kevin Sack, "Trying to Cut Welfare the Ohio Way," *New York Times*, April 3, 1995.

29. "Europe and the Underclass," *The Economist*, June 30, 1994, p. 21.

30. Valerie Polakow, "On a Tightrope without a Net," *Nation*, May 1, 1995, p. 592.

31. Mary Jo Bane and David T. Ellwood, *Welfare Realities: From Rhetoric to Reform* (Cambridge, Mass.: Harvard University Press, 1994), pp. 39–40. These figures take into account the likelihood of returning to the welfare system after a first spell.

32. Neil Gilbert, *Welfare Justice: Restoring Social Equity* (New Haven, Conn.: Yale University Press, 1995), p. 169.

33. Hilary Stout, "So Far, Efforts to Discourage Women on Welfare from Having More Children Yield Mixed Results," *Wall Street Journal*, March 27, 1995.

34. Janofsky.

35. Gary Burtless, "The Effect of Reform on Employment, Earnings, and Income," in *Welfare Policy for the 1990s*, ed. Phoebe Cottingham and David Ellwood (Cambridge, Mass.: Harvard University Press, 1989), pp. 103–40.

36. Douglas Besharov and Karen N. Gardiner, "Paternalism and Welfare Reform," *Public Interest*, no. 122 (Winter 1996): 70–84.

37. Richard L. Barclay, "The Poor? I Hire Them," *Wall Street Journal*, May 24, 1995. Barclay is vice president of Barclay Enterprises, in Riverside, California, which remanufactures telephone equipment.

38. Louis M. Nanni, "Not by Bread Alone," *American Enterprise* 6, no. 1 (January–February 1995): 60.

39. Quoted in Bane and Elwood, p. 9.

40. Peter Kilborn, "Home for Teen-Age Mothers Tries to Break Welfare Cycle," *New York Times*, October 31, 1996.

41. Quoted in Dana Milbank, "Michigan Now Relies on Churches to Help People Leave Welfare," *Wall Street Journal*, March 17, 1997.

42. Quoted in Robert Pear, "Some Charities Criticize Alexander's Welfare Plan," *New York Times*, February 24, 1996.

43. John C. Goodman, Gerald W. Reed, and Peter S. Ferrara, "Why Not Abolish the Welfare State?" National Center for Policy Analysis Policy Report no. 187, Dallas, October 1994, p. 25.

44. Independent Sector, *Giving and Volunteering in the United States*, 1996 edition (Washington: Independent Sector, 1996), pp. 1–10.

45. Quoted in Pear.

46. U.S. House of Representatives, Committee on Ways and Means, *Overview of Entitlement Programs: 1996 Green Book* (Washington: Government Printing Office, 1996), Tables 18.2, 18.3.

47. Karen W. Arenson, "Donations to Charities Rose 11% Last Year, Report Says," *New York Times*, May 23, 1996.

48. Independent Sector, p. 3.

49. Goodman, Reed, and Ferrara, pp. 3–4.

50. Stephen T. Ziliak, "The End of Welfare and the Contradiction of Compassion," *Independent Review* 1 (Spring 1996): 56.

51. Russell D. Roberts, "A Positive Model of Private Charity and Public Transfers," *Journal of Political Economy* 92 (1984): 143–45.

52. Ibid., quoting the AICP Annual Report for 1935–36.

Chapter 6

1. T. H. Marshall, *Citizenship and Social Class* (Cambridge: Cambridge University Press, 1950).

2. Jill Severn, "Amoral for America to Make Poor Grovel," *Seattle Post-Intelligencer*, October 6, 1995.

3. Bill Clinton, "A New Covenant," acceptance speech to the Democratic National Convention, July 16, 1992, in Bill Clinton and Al Gore, *Putting People First* (New York: Times Books, 1992), p. 226.

4. Robert Shapiro, "The End of Entitlement," *New Democrat*, July 1992, p. 16.

5. John Rawls, *A Theory of Justice* (Cambridge, Mass.: Harvard University Press, 1971), chaps. 2–3. This principle reflects the most common position among egalitarians: despite the moral presumption in favor of equality in wealth, income, and so forth, departures from equality are permissible, but only if they benefit others. Thus, the English writer R. H. Tawney wrote that "inequality of circumstance is regarded as reasonable, in so far as it is a necessary condition of securing the services which the community requires." R. H. Tawney, *Equality* (New York: Capricorn Books, 1952), p. 117. See also L. T. Hobhouse, *Liberalism* (1911; Oxford: Oxford University Press, 1964), p. 99.

6. Rawls, p. 276.

7. "Transcript of Keynote Address by Cuomo to the Convention," *New York Times*, July 17, 1984.

8. Michael Lerner, "Clinton's Economic Crusade," *Tikkun*, March–April 1993, p. 8.

9. Thomas W. Jones, "Social Security: Invaluable, Irreplaceable, and Fixable," *The Participant*, February 1996.

10. Henry Maine, *Ancient Law* (1861; New York: Dutton, 1917), pp. 99–100.

11. Gaston V. Rimlinger, *Welfare Policy and Industrialization in Europe, America and Russia* (New York: Wiley, 1971), p. 35.

12. Mary Ann Glendon, *Rights Talk* (New York: Free Press, 1991), p. 37.

13. Michael Sandel, *Liberalism and the Limits of Justice* (Cambridge: Cambridge University Press, 1982), p. 150.

14. Alasdair MacIntyre, *After Virtue* (Notre Dame, Ind.: Notre Dame University Press, 1984), p. 220.

15. Rawls, p. 101. Readers familiar with theoretical debates in political philosophy will find it odd that I have grouped Rawls with communitarians like Sandel and MacIntyre as exponents of the same line of thought. Rawls believes in a self that is distinct from its talents, character traits, convictions, and values; and that is precisely what communitarians deny. But Rawls's "unencumbered self" is a theoretical abstraction from the real identity of any actual individual, which consists in those attributes and which he agrees is largely created by social causes; and that is precisely what communitarians affirm. Rawls's "social contract" is merely a thought experiment, and it leads him to reject an actual society of contract in essentially the same way that communitarians would.

16. James Lindemann Nelson, "Routine Organ Donation: A Communitarian Organ Procurement Policy," *The Responsive Community*, Summer 1994, pp. 64, 68.

17. Will Marshall "The Politics of Reciprocity," *New Democrat* 4, no. 3 (July 1992): 6.

18. Glendon, p. 71.

19. Amitai Etzioni, *The Spirit of Community* (New York: Crown, 1993), pp. 5–9.

20. Neil Gilbert, *Welfare Justice* (New Haven, Conn.: Yale University Press, 1995), p. 165.

21. Marshall, pp. 78–79.

22. Ibid., p. 79.

23. "From the President's Address to Congress on Health Care," *New York Times*, September 23, 1993.

24. Quoted in Robert Pear, "Panel in Discord on the Financing of Social Security," *New York Times*, December 8, 1996.

25. Amitai Etzioni, "The Responsive Community: A Communitarian Perspective," *American Sociological Review*, February 1996, p. 3.

26. Charles Taylor, "Atomism," in *Philosophy and the Human Sciences* (Cambridge: Cambridge University Press, 1985), pp. 191.

27. Michael Walzer, "The Communitarian Critique of Liberalism," *Political Theory* 18, no. 1 (February 1990): 6–11.

28. Rawls, p. 4.

29. Robert Nozick, *Anarchy, State, and Utopia* (New York: Basic Books, 1974), pp. 188–89.

30. Marshall, pp. 58–59.

31. Tom Palmer, "What Rights Do We Have?" unpublished speech.

32. Gilbert, p. 165.

33. See, for example, R. Bruce Douglass, "The Renewal of Democracy and the Communitarian Prospect," *The Responsive Community*, Summer 1994. "[C]ommunitarians insist it is within our power to develop an alternative that does justice to our diversity. And this need not be some thin, least-common-denominator gruel either. We are quite capable of arriving at a set of shared purposes that reflects the best our several traditions have to offer. We can do it, that is, provided we are willing to learn anew how to talk with (not at) one another about the things that really matter" (p. 56). Douglass goes on, however, to discuss the difficulties of achieving consensus even about local issues facing people in the same city.

34. William C. Mitchell and Randy T. Simmons, *Beyond Politics: Markets, Welfare, and the Failure of Bureaucracy* (Boulder, Colo.: Westview, 1994), p. 171. Public choice theory holds that the operations of government are no less governed by the pursuit of individual self-interest than are the operations of the market.

35. On the fundamental distinction between concrete aims and abstract rules as methods of social coordination, see F. A. Hayek, *Rules and Order*, vol. 1 of *Law, Legislation and Liberty* (Chicago: University of Chicago Press, 1973), chaps. 1–2.

36. See F. A. Hayek, "The Use of Knowledge in Society," in *Individualism and Economic Order* (London: Routledge & Kegan Paul, 1948).

37. Jane Jacobs, quoted in John Tierney, "Brooklyn Could Have Been a Contender," *New York Times Magazine*, December 28, 1997.

38. "Summary of the 1997 Annual Social Security and Medicare Trust Fund Reports," *Social Security Bulletin* 60, no 2 (1997). The figure includes pension benefits paid by the Old-Age and Survivors Insurance Trust Fund and disability payments from the Disability Insurance Trust Fund. Figures used in this section refer to the combination of those programs (OASDI) and do not include Medicare benefits.

39. Gilbert, pp. 157–60. See also Michael Tanner, "Privatizing Social Security: A Big Boost for the Poor," Cato Institute Social Security Privatization Paper no. 4, July 26, 1996.

40. *Congressional Record* 102, 84th Cong., 2d sess., 1956, p. 15110.

41. Quoted in C. Eugene Steuerle and Jon M. Bakija, *Retooling Social Security for the 21st Century* (Washington: Urban Institute Press, 1994), p. 26.

42. "In posters, press releases, speeches, and newsreels prepared by social security officials, American workers were assured that the taxes they were paying were like insurance premiums. Having a social security card meant that one had opened 'an insurance account' with the government." W. Andrew Achenbaum, *Social Security: Visions and Revisions* (Cambridge: Cambridge University Press, 1986), p. 28.

43. Quoted in Arthur Schlesinger, *The Coming of the New Deal* (Boston: Houghton-Mifflin, 1958), pp. 308–9.

44. At the end of 1996, the Old-Age and Survivors Insurance and the Disability Insurance Trust Funds combined held $577 billion. Benefits paid from the trusts during 1996 were $354 billion.

45. "Summary of the 1997 Annual Social Security and Medicare Trust Fund Reports."

46. "Summary of the 1977 Annual Social Security and Medicare Trust Fund Reports," *Social Security Bulletin* 60, no. 2 (1977): 61, chart 3.

47. A. Haeworth Robertson, *The Big Lie: What Every Baby Boomer Should Know about Social Security and Medicare* (Washington: Retirement Policy Institute, 1997), pp. 40–41.

48. Melissa Hieger and William Shipman, "Common Objections to a Market-Based Social Security System: A Response," Cato Institute Social Security Paper no. 10, July 22, 1997, Appendix B.

49. For example, Peter Ferrara, *Social Security: The Inherent Contradiction* (San Francisco: Cato Institute, 1980); and A. Haeworth Robertson, *The Coming Revolution in Social Security* (Reston, Va.: Reston Publishing, 1981).

50. Chile's privatization of its pension system is one of the most successful and has served as a model for other countries. See José Piñero, "Empowering Workers: The Privatization of Social Security in Chile," Cato's Letter no. 10, Cato Institute, 1996.

51. William Shipman, "Retiring with Dignity: Social Security vs. Private Markets," Cato Institute Social Security Paper no. 2, August 14, 1995.

52. Mark Weinberger, "Social Security: Facing the Facts," Cato Institute Social Security Paper no. 3, April 10, 1996, p. 8. See also Philip Harmelink and Janet Speyer, "Social Security: Rates of Return and the Fairness of Benefits," *Cato Journal* 14, no. 1 (Spring–Summer 1994): 37–54.

53. Abram de Swaan, *In Care of the State: Health Care, Education and Welfare in Europe and the USA in the Modern Era* (New York: Oxford University Press, 1988), p. 166.

54. *Nestor v. Fleming*, 363 U.S. 603, 609–10 (1960).

55. Quoted in Charles Oliver, "The Death of Social Security," *Investor's Business Daily*, October 10, 1994.

56. Cf. Herbert Spencer, "The Coming Slavery," in *Herbert Spencer: Political Writings*, ed. John Offer (Cambridge: Cambridge University Press, 1994). "In ancient Greece the accepted principle was that the citizen belonged neither to himself nor to his family, but belonged to his city—the city being with the Greek equivalent to the community. And this doctrine, proper to a state of constant warfare, is a doctrine which socialism unawares re-introduces into a state intended to be purely industrial. The services of each will belong to the aggregate of all . . ." (p. 103).

Index

moral, 20
original conception of, 133
in political theory of the
Enlightenment, 16
principle as international standard,
15
as privileges, 133
in society of contract, 137
in United Nations Declaration of
Human Rights, 20–21
Rights, individual
in Declaration of Independence, 16
idea of, 15
incompatible with welfare rights,
64–65
Marx's opposition to, 47
in society of contract, 122–23, 128
See also Welfare rights
Rights, positive
acquiring, 131–32
within the family, 134
welfare entitlements as, 132
Right to life
core meaning of, 100
different interpretations of, 23
of individual, 96
Rimlinger, Gaston, 39, 54, 59, 123–24
Risk, associated with industrial
economy, 41–44
See also Economic risk
Roosevelt, Franklin D., 43, 141
bill of rights for welfare programs,
57
"Four Freedoms" speech, 48
on government as trustee of public
interest, 55–56
interpretation of right to life, 23
New Deal programs of, 4
request for welfare program bill of
rights, 57
on rights to economic goods, 20
on right to security, 50
on task of government, 160 n. 96
Rousseau, Jean-Jacques, 47
Rubinow, Irving R., 40

Samuels, Herbert, 49
Sandel, Michael, 124
Seager, Henry R., 40
Self, Rawls's concept of, 165 n. 15
Self-interest
according to the Bible, 92–93
gains from, 94
of individual, 31–32, 45–46, 66–67

modern concept of, 158 n. 59
pursuit of, 94–95
Senior, Nassau, 46
Shapiro, Robert, 120
Shapiro v. Thompson (1969), 18–19
Shipman, William, 143
Simmons, Randy, 136–37
Skinner, B. F., 52
Smith, Adam, 23, 46
Smith v. King (1968), 104
Social contract
fiction of, 134
of Rawls, 165 n. 15
Social engineering concept, 56–57
Social insurance
Bismarck's concept of, 12, 39–41
development in England, 40
opposition to German model of, 41
programs of Social Security Act, 4–5
Social Security Act in United States,
40
as welfare state transfer program,
26–27
Socialists
opponents of capitalism and
individualism, 47
on source of individual values, 51–52
Social Security Act (1935), 4
intent, 140
payroll tax funding for, 40
social insurance programs of, 4–5
Social Security system
benefits earned under, 141–42
changing terms of, 148
coming crisis in, 141–45
consumption by (1996), 139–40
idea of collective social solidarity
under, 127–28
payroll tax paid to trust fund, 40, 140
proposal to privatize, 13
rising costs of, 11
Social Security trust fund
current balance, 142
draw-down trigger, 142–43
investments and uses of, 142–43
payroll tax to fund, 40, 140
Society
communitarian model of, 135
conception of classical liberals, 31–32,
55, 128
as concept of giant family, 149
as family, 134
measure of good, 95
political and civil, 13

About the Author

David Kelley is founder and, since 1990, executive director of the Institute for Objectivist Studies, a leading center for research and education in Objectivism, the philosophy originated by Ayn Rand, world famous author of *The Fountainhead* and *Atlas Shrugged*, among other works.

His many articles on social issues and public policy have appeared in *Barron's, Harpers, The Sciences, Harvard Business Review,* and elsewhere. He also lectures widely and is a frequent talk show guest. He was recently featured on John Stossel's ABC-TV special, "Greed."

A well-known philosopher, teacher, and writer, David Kelley earned his Ph.D. in philosophy from Princeton University in 1975. He has since taught philosophy, cognitive sciences, and other courses at Vassar College and Brandeis University.

Kelley's books include *The Evidence of the Senses*, a treatise on perception; *The Art of Reasoning*, a widely used college logic textbook; *Truth and Toleration*, an essay on the principles of intellectual exchange; and *Unrugged Individualism: The Selfish Basis of Benevolence.*

Cato Institute

Founded in 1977, the Cato Institute is a public policy research foundation dedicated to broadening the parameters of policy debate to allow consideration of more options that are consistent with the traditional American principles of limited government, individual liberty, and peace. To that end, the Institute strives to achieve greater involvement of the intelligent, concerned lay public in questions of policy and the proper role of government.

The Institute is named for *Cato's Letters*, libertarian pamphlets that were widely read in the American Colonies in the early 18th century and played a major role in laying the philosophical foundation for the American Revolution.

Despite the achievement of the nation's Founders, today virtually no aspect of life is free from government encroachment. A pervasive intolerance for individual rights is shown by government's arbitrary intrusions into private economic transactions and its disregard for civil liberties.

To counter that trend, the Cato Institute undertakes an extensive publications program that addresses the complete spectrum of policy issues. Books, monographs, and shorter studies are commissioned to examine the federal budget, Social Security, regulation, military spending, international trade, and myriad other issues. Major policy conferences are held throughout the year, from which papers are published thrice yearly in the *Cato Journal*. The Institute also publishes the quarterly magazine *Regulation*.

In order to maintain its independence, the Cato Institute accepts no government funding. Contributions are received from foundations, corporations, and individuals, and other revenue is generated from the sale of publications. The Institute is a nonprofit, tax-exempt, educational foundation under Section 501(c)3 of the Internal Revenue Code.

CATO INSTITUTE
1000 Massachusetts Ave., N.W.
Washington, D.C. 20001